How to get out of debt and
stay out of debt

Aber Publishing

Aussie, Aussie Readers

Back to the Black

The Adult Skills Series

The Adult Numeracy Series

Hey Thompson: Developing self-esteem and resilience in secondary school students

Self Esteem: a Manual for Mentors

Contentious Issues

Life Skills: Bullying

Life Skills: Family Relationships

Life Skills: Grief, Illness and other Issues

Life Skills: Self Esteem and Values

Enhancing Self Esteem in the Adolescent

Survival Teen Island

Understanding the Numbers:
The first steps in managing your money

Understanding Maths:
Basic Mathematics Explained

Books to Improve Your Life

Dr Graham Lawler's
Back to the Black

How to get out of debt and stay out of debt

Dr Graham Lawler

For Jeff and Margaret Bestwick and Kate and Graeme King
– thank you for your friendship for over twenty years
and as always
for Jude – without you I would never have written a word.

ISBN: 978-184285-141-8

© 2009 Graham Lawler

Website: www.aber-publishing.co.uk

Printed and bound in Europe

Contents

Preface

Writing a book is actually a team affair and I need to place on record my thanks to Jude, JG and also Ray Kroc.

Now Ray Kroc is something of a hero of mine because he had an incredible insight that few others have had. You see Ray Kroc saw something in the 1950s that he knew would work. He was a salesman and he went to see the Dick and Mac McDonald to sell them a milk shake machine. To cut a long story short, it was Ray Kroc who developed the McDonald fast food outlet business that you can see in every town across the world. What Ray Kroc did was invent a system where, using school kids on minimum wage, he could create a product to the same standard. This system works anywhere, at any time as long as you keep to the system. Don't change it – because *it works.*

That is what I have developed in the 'Back to the black' system. I want you to treat this the same way as Ray Kroc asked his employees to treat the burger system, don't change it, just use it, because it does work. This is a system that is designed to get you out of debt and into credit, or as we used to say 'out of the red and back to the black'. I examined a number of other debt repayment systems but they all lacked one thing, they were all foreign and therefore a poor fit for Britain. So I determined what was needed was a British system and that is what I have designed. I know from personal experience that it does work and so I recommend it highly to you. You can be debt free, you can have savings and you can get 'Back to the black'.

Younger readers may not be aware of this, but historically in the UK bank statements were printed using either black print or red ink. If you received your bank statement with red print, you were in debt. This became known as 'being in the red'. If your statement was in black print, you were in credit or had money in the bank, this was known as 'being in the black'. So it became a common phrase when saving and paying off debt to say that one was 'getting out of the red and back to the black', this is why we called this book, *Back to the Black*.

Graham Lawler

1 **You and Money**

I want to change your life.

Have you ever wondered 'Where does all my money go?' or heard someone say, 'Money just slips through my fingers'? Then welcome to the club, we have all been where you are. I was once asked, 'Graham, does money speak to you?' I said 'Yes, it usually says goodbye'. We can joke about it, but the fact remains that there are certain truths in the world. Number one, you are where you are in life because of the decisions you made that led you there.

If you are reading this book, then it suggests to me that you do not necessarily like being where you are (neither did I). In this book (probably the most open book I have ever written), I will divulge certain facts that have happened in my life and their outcome, but my aim in this book is simple, **I want to change your life**. I want you to wake up in the morning in a home that you love and know that it is all yours because you have paid for it. I want you to relax and feel confident as you face the day because you know that you have savings. In the event of something bad in life happening, you have funds to see you through and, most of all, I want you to have the satisfaction of knowing that you own everything in your life. Does that surprise you? Are you one of these cynics who says 'Oh yes, Graham and excuse me, but how am I going to do that?' Well, if you are, it may surprise you that I do not blame you.

I started my adult life in debt and went on to live for over 20 years with debt. As I write this I have no personal debt. I left college in 1981 (Chester College, now Chester University) and was one of Thatcher's graduate unemployed. Eventually, after six weeks of unemployment (and spending the summer on the buses as a bus conductor on Rhyl prom), I managed to get a supply job teaching in Rhyl. Supply teaching is temporary teaching, there is no security. Due to a convoluted route I left there and ended up in Leicestershire where I taught for a number of years and then moved to Somerset. During this time I was racking up debt. There was always a car debt, there were house moves, then the inevitable home contents that wore out and needed replacement. So it went on and on for over 20 years until we (by now I was married) had had enough.

Both my wife, Judith, and I were at the time doing part-time PhD research degrees so we were learning how to research. We went online and found a foreign programme. While it was good, it did not answer all our problems – well after all, this is the UK and we do things differently here. So bearing that in mind, we developed the British Back to the black programme and we would like to invite you to engage with this programme. If you follow our advice, you will sleep better at night, you will clear your debts, you will own your own home in a few short years and you will feel far more confident. It has worked for us and it will work for you.

Becoming debt free

You do not need a PhD to understand the mathematics in this book and you certainly do not need one to understand finance (and I should know because I have a PhD) but what you do need to have is the desire to be debt free. You need to want to wake up in the morning with the knowledge that your home is paid for, that you own it and that your account in the bank is in the black, not in the red. In order to achieve that you will need some discipline and this is what this book is about. My good friend Nigel, from South Wales has achieved this great state in life. He said to me, 'Graham, it is a great feeling to wake up in the morning and know you own everything and owe nothing. It is lovely.' I can still hear his lilting South Walian accent as he said this, when we were staying in a hotel in Germany whilst at the Frankfurt International Bookfair. This is the feeling I want you to enjoy. I am not totally there myself, my debts are paid off although I do have a mortgage.

However, in five years my wife and I have turned what was a debt mountain into a savings pot. We were in debt for thousands and I couldn't afford to take her on a £1,500 holiday yet I was spending £1,500 on computer magazines. What a dummy!

There are no complicated secrets needed to bury the debt monster but it is sometimes a long haul. Trust me, in the long run it will be well worth it. This may well take you a few years, on average in the USA, where the model for this system comes from, it takes five and seven years, but that is nothing compared to a lifetime in debt.

Just because you may be in debt now doesn't mean you have been full of wild abandon, it doesn't mean you have been carelessly reckless and deliberately created a family debt crisis. Very often, a consistent pattern of a small amount of over-spending leads to a serious problem and that is what we can help to change. So, if you want to get out of debt and stay out of debt, if you want to transform your debt into wealth, then this book and this series of books will show you how to do it.

Transforming your debt into wealth is the key to a great financial future. This system will show you how to prioritise and pay off your debts and cope with emergencies so you will never need to borrow again. That is true financial freedom. You deserve to make yourself secure financially, you deserve to feel secure, this is all possible and that is what this book will show you. Don't expect the state to step in and feed you when you are elderly, there is not enough cash in the cupboard, the shelves are bare.

In the UK we are a rapidly ageing community. Traditionally, when National Insurance payments have been made, we have been told that the money paid in, is for our old age pension. In reality, that money goes to pay the *present* pension generation. It is not being saved or invested on our behalf, it is being spent to support pensioners *now*. However, there is a rising problem, the number of young people is decreasing so that means the tax burden per person has to increase to pay for elderly care. This could cause long-term social problems. This is a real social time bomb that could explode in the future, because who is to say that by 2020, young people will be prepared to work and pay taxes to keep older people?

This is why I keep coming back to the only realistic solution and that is to have a secure future you need to plan and cater for yourself. That way *you* are taking control, *you* are in charge and *you* will be the one who ultimately benefits. But does that mean it is all doom and gloom? The entrepreneur and TV dragon Duncan Bannantyne advocates putting life on hold for a while if you are building a new business. Should you do the same thing whilst paying off debts? Absolutely not.

Journal	In *Understanding the numbers*, the first book in this series, I advocated using a journal. The purpose of this is to get you thinking. It is important that you interact with the information in this book, so we will use the same approach in this book.

Splash the cash

Amanda Bowman is a radio broadcaster in the East Midlands and I was fortunate enough to be interviewed on her lunchtime show. At the time, I was promoting the first edition of *Understanding the numbers* and Amanda made a point. She said something along the lines, 'It is all right you talking about saving money but you are taking the fun out of life.'

This was a fair point and so we have accommodated it in this plan because Amanda was right. Life is not, in our view anyway, a rehearsal. As the TV celebrity Noel Edmonds said in his book, 'We are not here for a long time, we are here for a good time'.

And so it must be, we must have a good time. But that does not means we have to spend every last penny or cent of our earnings. It does not mean we need to be out every Friday night splashing the cash.

It is not the case that you have to become a 'tight wad', you can enjoy life in this system but do you really have to go out on Friday, Saturday and Sunday evenings and splash the cash? Why not get your mates over to your house and share a DVD. Before I was married, my good mate Colin and his mate Ian and me would often roll up at one of our houses, usually Colin's and watch a movie. OK so we didn't meet many girls that way but we didn't spend £100 on a night out. Before you gasp at £100, it is actually quite easy to spend this amount of cash. I was in London in 2005 and was charged £5 for a ½pint of beer then, in other words beer was £10 a pint at that particular place. I didn't go there again. If you go to a top club it can cost a door fee well in excess of £10 just to get in. We know one club in England which charged £50 for men to get in but women got in for free, hmmmm, equal opportunities laws seemed not to work here.

The point is you can have a good time without splashing cash that you do not own. You can meet new people without spending other people's money to do so. If you are in trouble financially this book will help but go to Citizens Advice, they will put you in touch with support agencies. This is especially true if you are on your own. I remember when I was broke and alone and it was a very scary time. One way to meet new people is to join voluntary groups in your area. When I was single I joined hospital radio and met some great people, many of whom I am still friends with today. Other organisations include Rotaract (young Rotary), and Rotary itself. What about a talking newspaper? They always need volunteers to record news for the blind. What about meals on wheels for the elderly and infirm?

Journal Write down five places in your location where you can go for free. Find three organisations that you can join to get involved in voluntary work and meet people. These are all places where you can go and have a good time without spending a fortune. Life is not a rehearsal, this is it friend so you must enjoy but you must enjoy within your means. There is no law that says you have to do without but you have to be able to pay for it. When the credit crunch that started in 2007 hit home, we heard of a city trader who had enjoyed the high life for the last five years. This young man had worked hard and had earned £85,000 a year and . . . had spent the lot. How do you spend £85,000 in one year? Well actually it is quite easy if you live in London and eat out every night and go to expensive restaurants and clubs. But the young man concerned lost his job in the credit crunch and had zero savings. He had to claim jobseekers allowance and was that a shock to his system.

How does money make you feel?

I asked this of a class of 15-year-olds in a school in the North of the UK and the answers ranged from 'excited' to 'scared'. These young people were from ordinary backgrounds; some lived in families where there was no breadwinner, occasionally the single parent/guardian was claiming unemployment benefit. Yet every single one of them saw money in a different way except for one thing. In a class full of 30 teenagers, not one of them believed they could ever be rich, without winning the lottery.

Just think about that for a moment, not one of these kids thought they could be rich. Yet the reality is that in the twenty-first century there has never been an easier time to become rich. In 2007, according to the BBC, the UK had 21 billionaires (depending on where you look on the BBC website it also says 40 billionaires); the writer JK Rowling is worth a reputed £280 million. The writer Jackie Collins has a reputed £60 million, Hans Rausing the food packaging magnate is reported to be worth £4.8 billion, formula one chief Bernie Ecclestone is reported to be worth £2.4 billion, and I could go on. I can tell you that most of these estimates are probably wrong, for instance I mentioned above that JK Rowling was worth £280 million above, but according to another page on the BBC website she is worth over £400 million from the huge success of the Harry Potter phenomenon. So how come these people have all this money and ordinary folks:

a)   don't have it; and

b)   don't believe they can ever have it?

It is because of the way they have been brought up to think about money. The truth is that the way you think affects the amount of money in your life. I am not a millionaire but in the last four years by applying certain principles, principles which I will share with you in this book, I have cleared major debts and turned them into substantial savings and, by following this programme, I have every intention of becoming a millionaire and am not ashamed to say so.

I want to make one thing clear, as I said in *Understanding the Numbers*, I have been there. I know what it is like to be in debt. I have had the sleepless nights and the worry, I know what it is like to have to contact your debtors and say 'Er, sorry can we just have 30 more days' and I want to help you through them.

Jude, my beloved other half, went through a similar emotional journey. Jude had been brought up to believe that a wife's role was as the home maker and to that end a good home maker always keeps a well stocked larder. It was great, whenever I wanted something nice to snack on, there was plenty to choose from but we were spending money on food that we didn't need and my weight shot up to over 100 kilos (over 17 stone), clearly this was unhealthy and I now weigh a lot less. Jude realised that we only needed to buy enough food for this week and that next week we could go back to the supermarket and buy again. This was a significant shift in her thinking and had a huge effect on our cashflow (more of that later) and on my waistline. The point is Jude's emotional response to her role as my partner was to ensure that we had enough food in the house so that the larder was always well stocked.

Now we sometimes run out of say, eggs, before the end of the week but there is always something to make a meal with, even if there are no eggs. So, by just altering her emotional belief, Jude actually performed a greater service for us as a family, (and completed a great emotional journey herself) she cut the bills and we still ate well (and healthily).

So our emotional response to money and the way we think about money affects the way we respond.

We all have an emotional response to money. George was a teacher who later went on to become an advisor for a local authority in England. He once said to me 'Nobody ever made money honestly'. This shows a lot about the way he thinks about money. To George, having money is a reflection of poor character, it is undesirable, since who would wish to be associated with those kinds of people. It was no surprise when he later said 'I have never had more than £1,000 saved in my life.'

George has failed to understand his own emotional feelings to money. No doubt this could be a response to his childhood but, remember, it is not where we are coming from that matters, it is where we are going to.

The emotional feelings that those young people in the school mentioned above had for money was that they really felt uncomfortable in controlling it, in that sense they feared money. How we think about something affects how we react to it. This happens in music. Think about what happened in the 1960s in Liverpool and in Detroit. Both cities produced fabulous music. Liverpool produced the Mersey Sound, first of all with the Beatles then (the list is legendary), Gerry and the Pacemakers, Cilla Black, The Merseybeats names just a few. Similarly, in Detroit there were dozens of groups and singers who produced beautiful soul music including Ray Charles, Sam Cooke, Little Richard and, of course, the legendary James Brown. OK – was there something in the water in Liverpool or Detroit that affected so many people and made them want to make such great music? I don't think so. The most likely explanation is quite simple. Imagine you are in Liverpool and a couple of friends called John and Paul start a group and begin to be successful, why shouldn't you do the same? If John and Paul and George and (eventually) Ringo can start a group why can't you? What if you work in the cloakroom of The Cavern in Liverpool and your name is Priscilla White? It isn't too great a step to becoming a singer and becoming the highly successful and admired entertainer that we know in the UK as Cilla Black is it?

The same is true in the US. If you were walking down a street in Detroit and heard black harmony singing, well it wouldn't be difficult to knock on Mr Berry Gordy's door with your group now would it? Now apply the same thinking to money. The same processes apply. To be a pop singer in Liverpool or a soul singer in Detroit you would do what the successful people like the Beatles and Cilla did or like Ray Charles or Sam Cooke did.

What if you thought about money the way rich people do? What if you did what the rich do, wouldn't you get the same or similar results? You bet you would.

Understanding your emotional response to money?

This is something that I want you to take a moment to think about. Are you in control of your money? Because you are reading this book, it seems likely that you have debt and frankly, that means the answer is 'no'.

Pause for a moment, it hurts doesn't it? It hurt me. Here I was a man in my early 40s, a mathematics teacher, and figures were not really a problem, yet I was afraid that I couldn't control the money in my life. Before Jude and I married I had often had to go to the bank to secure a loan because I simply couldn't manage. I was living on tomorrow's money. Then two things happened that made me so angry, that I determined to do something about it.

First of all, when I met Jude I knew there was a spark there between us and I thought I had better start acting responsibly, so I contacted a well known UK high street bank and asked them for a savings plan. This was simply because I was spending every penny I earned. Yes, I could justify the spending, or so I thought, but the reality was I had no savings – absolutely nothing. So I thought that if I paid into a savings plan then there would be a nest egg and that if we were to get together (as we did), then I would need a savings plan. So I bought a product from this particular bank. I paid in every month for ten years – I never missed. But when payout time came, instead of getting a nice cheque, they actually paid me back £400 less than I had paid them. The net effect was that for ten years from the age of 32 I had given them my money and they charged me £400 for the privilege of doing so. I was shocked and outraged that such a well-established company could behave in this way but it was a lesson. It was also the reason why in *Understanding the Numbers* that I wrote **'Banks are your enemy'**.

Following the credit crunch that started in 2007, it is now well known that banks in the UK (along with those in many other countries) have had to be bailed out by their respective government. In other words, you and I paid, through our taxes, for the stupidity of the bankers who lent money to people who could not pay and then sold on that debt. What is not so well known in Britain is that, according to a newspaper report, one of the major high street banks in the run up to Christmas 2008 spent £100,000 on Christmas parties for staff. Well, excuse me for being a Scrooge, but this is the equivalent of five years' work for an ordinary person and, frankly, did the banks deserve such Christmas treat? Before you fire off emails telling me what a miserable so-and-so I am, think on, who paid for those parties? It was you and me, either through our taxes or through our credit payments. Remember, they spent in *one week*, what you or I would earn in *five years*. As I said, banks are your enemy.

The second thing that happened that affected my attitude to money was the mortgage mis-selling scandal of the 1980s. I was suckered by the promises of an endowment mortgage. It was the 'modern way' to pay off your mortgage. I was promised that there would be enough cash to pay off the mortgage and I could retire with a nest egg, enough to buy a boat (not for me, thank you) or a camper van/SUV (yes, please) and travel. I would be comfortable for the rest of my life…**big lie**. However, I did complain to the banking ombudsman about this and got a sizeable amount in compensation.

Couple this with the reality I faced when I determined what my emotional response to money was. I had been brought up to believe that:

a   you work hard at school and get a good education;

b   you go to college and get a degree;

c   you are comfortable for the rest of your life.

This is old-century thinking. I will keep banging on about this because I need you to understand that whilst a and b are important in this equation, they do not necessarily lead to c. I did a and b, but c did not happen. I did not have the lifestyle that I had been led to believe would happen.

This is what made me determined to take control of my own affairs. After all, if this was how the so-called 'experts' behaved, then I could hardly do worse. Richard Farleigh, formerly one of the Dragons on BBC TV's *Dragons Den* makes a point in his book about experts and the markets. It is virtually the same point as I am making here, although in a different context. Many so-called experts are just commentators – they are simply giving their opinion and their opinion is often not as valid as your own opinion. Don't be impressed because someone calls themselves an expert, it could be that they have been on a course lasting a week or maybe no course at all.

CASE STUDY

One salesman tried to sell me a health policy. The deal was that I would pay £100 per month for three years and then, at the end of three years, I would get £1,000. Sounds good? I bought the same product for £6 per month (six pounds) against £100. Let's do some simple mathematics:

3 years is 36 months

36 × 100 =	**£3,600**
Subtract £1,000 leaves cost of product at	**£2,600**
36 months × 6 =	**£216**

Look at the difference for the same product – incredible isn't it! I nearly paid over ten times the price for the same product and I would have given them £1,000 of my money on a free loan for three years.

Robbie Williams

Our emotional response to money can sabotage the way we live. In a very honest interview the pop star Robbie Williams told the TV journalist Michael Parkinson that sometimes he behaves in way that starts to destroy what he has achieved because there is part of him that doesn't believe he should have it. Robbie Williams is an ordinary boy from the English Midlands who has a super talent and has developed it; he does deserve his success, although he sometimes thinks otherwise.

Are you like that? Is there a part of you that doesn't believe you are entitled to be comfortable or to be debt free? If so, this is something that you will need to work on. Believe me when I tell you that you are entitled. You are entitled to sleep well at night, in your own home that is paid for, having eaten well that evening and knowing that the bank account with your name on, is healthily in the black.

CASE STUDY

As I mentioned above, I was a teacher. If you are reading this outside the UK you may not be aware that teachers in the UK have a teachers' superannuation. The same salesman mentioned above tried to sell me a private pension plan. I contacted my teachers' union for advice and they told me to stay put. The salesman called me a fool to my face. How easy it would have been to cave in. My response to my family was that a barrister was advising me; this salesman had been on a week's course.

Now we have again seen another mis-selling scandal that emanates from the 1980s where people were tricked into converting their pensions into the private product available and they have lost out. It has been so bad that many companies have been forced to pay compensation.

By understanding how you feel about money and also understanding some basic mathematics, you can usually do as a good job as the so-called experts and very often better.

In the last four years, we have gone from being in debt to clearing our debts and having money to invest. You could do the same.

Journal	What is your emotional response to money? In your journal write down how you feel about your financial situation today. I am not asking you to number crunch, don't think of the bills you owe, the money you earn, the money you spend, instead think of the feelings associated with money for you. You need to address your feelings honestly. How does it feel not to have enough money? Write down how it feels to be in debt. You might surprise yourself with the underlying feelings.

Look carefully at what you have written, these are not just words they are truths. Highlight any emotional words, like fear, anger, jealousy, because they explain how you feel about money. You must confront your feelings. Don't hide anything or kid yourself – this is important.

I hinted at my own emotional response to money above, now I want to tell you exactly how I felt. I mentioned:

a   you work hard at school and get a good education;

b   you go to college and get a degree;

c   you are comfortable for the rest of your life.

For me the equation simply did not work.

$a + b = c$ is rubbish, it did not happen to me. If this equation works, how come when I went to college and got a degree and my mate went to catering college and became a chef, but he is now a millionaire and I am not? (Not yet anyway, I am working on it.) In all fairness to him, he is a millionaire because he built up a good business in care homes and he deserves his success.

> **EDUCATION IS VITAL**
> Don't get me wrong, education is vital, it is *not* a waste of time. There is a certain so-called expert who encourages people to leave school and get started in the 'university of life'. This is a big error. Educated people live longer, they have better relationships, they enjoy life and they are wealthier than uneducated people. In researching this book I have come across stories of people who have followed the advice of these so-called experts and quit school and their jobs to start a business only to go bankrupt. Going to school and learning and then getting further and higher education is an investment in you, it is vital and is not a waste of time.

My response to the a+b=c equation, my underlying emotion, was anger. I felt betrayed. I had done my bit, done what I was told would be the right thing to do, sacrificed lots of 'now' time, (when friends would call asking me to go out I had to decline because I was writing essays) and yet I still had no tangible benefit in terms of increased money. So I believed I was 'entitled' and therefore bought myself 'treats'. Now it won't surprise you that as a writer I like books but I was buying books like they were going out of fashion. At one time I belonged to five book clubs – trust me – nobody needs to belong to five book clubs. All of this was because I was angry that the system had, in my view, let me down. Look at what was happening, my emotional cloud of anger was affecting my rational thinking and I was buying books that gave me an **emotional boost**. I still like books and still buy them but on a spending plan (more of that later) but here the books were to make me *feel* better.

I have seen the same thing time and time again with other people buying clothes. One couple, Helen and Mark went shopping every week for clothes because it 'made them feel better'. Helen's wedding dress in the 1980s cost over £600 yet a friend of mine, Kate said 'I could have made that for £10'. Mark's designer suit cost £180 at a time when off-the-peg suits were available for £50 and take home pay for a teacher was about £300 per month. This was a couple who were feeding their emotional need by buying clothes, it made them *feel* better. Helen and Mark were buying clothes they simply couldn't afford. In the end Helen was called into the bank and her credit cards were cut up in front of her. Imagine the humiliation of that, you really do not want to go there.

For me it was books, for them it was clothes, but essentially it was the same thing. We wanted to feel better. What is it for you?

The point is this: by understanding your emotional response to money, you can begin to understand why you spend and that can be the first step to getting out of debt. Your behaviour is a response to your emotional state; it can cloud your judgement and wreck your finances.

Forgive yourself and others

So you have to make a choice. I have been honest with you about my own errors. I was a book junkie when I couldn't really afford it. My thinking was clouded and I bet you are in a similar situation, otherwise, why are you reading this book? To start anew you have to do something that demands a lot of you. You have to forgive yourself and those who have transgressed you.

What do we mean by forgiveness? I want to make sure that I am communicating this clearly. Forgiveness does not mean 'Oh, it doesn't matter.' It seems to me that far too many people put themselves down and allow others to walk all over them. If someone has done you wrong, you are important so when you forgive someone, it must mean that:

a   the transgression was wrong and that you were rightly
    hurt and/or damaged, but

b   you will take *no action* against them.

This, to me, is true forgiveness. It means that you remain
rightly with your self esteem intact since you are not letting
the world and his dog walk over you. But, on the other
hand, you are being powerful by saying to the transgressor,
'What you did was wrong, but I am of such a powerful
personality that I have decided I will take no action against
you.'

Look at how powerful that makes you. You have risen so
high you are now towering above the transgressors. Pause
for a moment. Doesn't it make you powerful? You bet it
does!

You also have to forgive yourself. Many years ago when I
dreamed of being a writer I took a job in an office in
Somerset where I was employed to work with a group of
people. Right from the start things started to go awry. The
group dynamics were totally wrong and one of the women
took an instant dislike to me. She made it her life's task to
create trouble for me and I do mean trouble. Things would
go missing off my desk; daily there were rows; I was
verbally abused; coffee would be made for everyone else but
I was regularly deliberately left out. I was once even
physically hit (though it didn't hurt much because she was
so small and I am a big man). But I stuck it for three years
because quite simply I needed a job and was afraid I would
struggle to get another one.

The point I am making is that the behaviour of some of
those people in that office was disgraceful, but I have
moved on. I have forgiven them, especially the woman who
tried to make my life hell. That does not mean I am saying
what they did was nothing. It does not mean I am simply
saying 'Oh, never mind, it didn't matter', because it did

matter. But what I am saying is that I have risen above that scenario and although what they did was wrong, I will take no action against them.

One person was professional and genuinely pleasant towards me but others were not. She is the only one, as far as I am aware, who is still involved in any sort of publishing. One guy, a boss, argued with me because I wanted to keep minutes of meetings and he would not allow it, that was the level of his thinking. I hope he is happy with his lot and I have forgiven him for how he transgressed towards me but he was wrong in how he behaved.

Finally, I have forgiven myself. Let me explain. I stuck to this miserable job (and it was miserable, we were working on a project that due to extremely poor management failed) because I didn't have the faith to believe I could run my own company, which is exactly what I do now. In other words I stuck to that job because despite how miserable it was, it was a job and a job was better than no job, right? **Wrong**.

Get this big time, **people, money, things** are what matters.

I have forgiven myself for being afraid and for not thinking I could make it. In all fairness, after three years of that sort of treatment I wasn't the most confident of people at that time but I did strike out on my own and ten years later we have been extremely successful. We have a good company, I have written a number of books, including some books for the BBC and the UK's Channel 4 TV company and have had some lovely responses from readers. I have also learnt a major lesson, put people first, then money and then possessions. Think about it, it does make sense.

However, it is very easy to get this wrong. I once worked in an organisation for a six-month period where I met Fred. Fred was a great guy, a senior manager who was professional and reliable. What I didn't know was that Fred was being abused daily by his bosses. This went on for a number of years until he could take the strain no longer; he left a note for his wife and then went into the countryside and killed himself. (The most disgusting aspect of this situation in my view was the press report that his boss had publicly stated he was unaware that there was a problem. I know from the time I spent there that six staff had been away with stress-related illness, so how could he not know).

Fred was depressed and had lost sight of the fact that people matter more than money or things and that he mattered the most. He couldn't cope with his job but could see no way out. He had been in the same job since 1979 and had about 12 years to work before retirement; to him this was a prison sentence. Had he resigned, he didn't know what else to do. In truth he could have been a bus driver or wagon driver, or worked in a supermarket or done a whole host of other things like selling fruit and vegetables on a market stall. Yes, he would have taken a huge cut in pay and his family would have felt the financial pressure, but Fred would still be alive today. He is now dead and I bet his family feels the pain of that emotional hole where he used to be in the family and will continue to do so for a lifetime.

Later in the book I will talk about planning your future. I want to make something clear. I do not advocate, as some writers do, giving up your job without any thought. It is something that has to be planed for. *But*, if you are in a similar position to Fred, then you need to take emergency action. No job is worth a life and if you are miserable in your job then start planning today to improve things. Depression is an illness and is nothing to be ashamed of either as an individual or as a family. If you are depressed or you think someone in the family is depressed, the first thing is to see your doctor. It may be that you need some time off work to see things in a better way. It may be you need to re-design your life and we will talk about this later in this book. The important thing is to rise above your fears and focus on the problem. You are not the problem, your situation is the problem and you can improve your situation.

As I said above: people, money, things.

Today tell someone you care about them and make sure you forgive yourself for any past wrongs when it comes to money. I am not the person I was and you are not the person you were. You can grow as a person and you have the right to be successful, you have the right to sleep well in a home you own and to know there is money in the bank.

Right now that is out of the way, let's get on with it.

2 Spiralling Debt and You

What is the difference between a debt and an expense?

A debt is something that can be paid off, an expense is an ongoing situation. So buying food for the family is an expense, buying a car is a debt. Think about it. You will always need to eat so this is an expense but there will come a time when the car loan is paid off and therefore this is a debt. In fact, what the credit card companies ideally want is for you to have converted all of your debt into ongoing expenses, because that way they make money from you big time!

What is debt?

Debt is the money you owe to someone else. It may seem silly but many adults simply do not understand this idea. In effect, when you are in debt, you are spending someone else's money, it doesn't belong to you, it is not yours, they are lending it to you to spend, usually with the agreement that you will pay it back with interest. Interest is the fee you pay for using their money. So, when you have borrowed money from a person or an institution, you are in debt. But it starts to get trickier than this simple definition.

The secured loan

When something is secured, it means it is safe. To secure a boat on the riverside, you would tie it securely to its moorings. When you secure a loan, you are making it safe, *for the lender*, not for you. You are making sure the lender is free from the risk of losing his or her money.

This is usually by providing collateral. Collateral in its true meaning means something that runs alongside something else. In money terms, collateral is what you use to free the lender from risk. In other words, you enter an agreement that means that you agree, if anything goes wrong, that the lender gets something you own if you cannot pay the money back. A good example of this is a mortgage on a house. A mortgage is a loan to buy a house. If you fail to make the payments to the mortgage lender, you can have the house re-possessed. In other words, the lender can take it from you and then sell it to get their money back, that is how they are secure, how their risk is removed. There have been cases in the UK of houses being repossessed and the house then being sold off incredibly cheaply to regain the owed money. In the long run this is silly. It means the family are evicted and often end up in bed and breakfast accommodation. This has a huge cost to the state. But in fairness the lender needs to get their money back so, as we shall see later, it makes a lot more sense for borrowers and lenders to talk to each other and to find a way forward, together.

So the collateral is security for the lender. When the debt is paid off in full, the lender returns the collateral to you. It doesn't matter if it is a pawnbroker or a bank, it is still the same, you borrow money and pay it back with interest. Remember interest is a fee that you pay on top of the money you have borrowed. It is worth noting that the collateral that is offered against the loan has to have the same value as the loan, no one is seriously going to accept collateral that is worth less. If you need persuading about this, try buying a Rolls-Royce and offering a pencil as collateral on the loan, you will not get far.

The numbers don't affect the facts. It is totally irrelevant if you have borrowed £5, £50 or £5,000,000, they are still loans and collateral is still collateral whether it is a gold watch or a gold Rolls-Royce.

There is an apocryphal story about a businessman who took out a loan for three weeks and gave his Rolls-Royce as collateral. He drove the car into the bank's car park and handed over the keys and went off with his money. Three weeks later he repaid the money and the accrued interest, which was a few hundred pounds. The bank manager asked him what he had done with the money in such a short time and was amazed when the answer came back as 'nothing'. The businessman said, 'I just needed a secure area to park my car whilst I was on holiday and where else can I park a Roller securely in London for this price?'

Car loans work in the same manner. If I buy a new Ford for £16,000, I put down £5,000 of my own money and borrow the remainder from either the bank or Ford themselves. In order to be allowed to have the financing, I sign a document that means if I do not pay for the car, then I forfeit all rights to it and it reverts to the lender. In other words, the lender can snatch back the car and then resell it to recover their money. If I default on this car loan, yes I would lose the car but I would also lose the debt, because I no longer owe the money to the lender.

So debt is:

1	any amount of borrowed cash that is borrowed unsecured, i.e. without collateral;
2	any credit that is extended to you;
3	any service that you have received without paying for it at the time.

Look at these examples:

- Many people borrow from friends or family regularly, say £20 to tide them over to the following week.

- When you borrow from the bank to tide you over.

- When you borrow from parents or grandparents to buy something.

- When you buy fuel for your car using your MasterCard.

- When you take someone out to dinner and pay for it using a Visa card.

- When you fly to Spain for a long weekend and max out your credit card to do it.

- When you buy the groceries with money lent by your brother or sister.

They are all debts.

All of these people or organisations are owed money by you. They have taken no collateral from you. The credit card company can't 'undo' the flight you took to Spain, or take the fuel out of the tank of your car. **You owe them**.

I need you to think about debt, so I want to take you back to the 1980s for a moment. In the 1980s I was a teacher in Leicester and lived in Loughborough. I needed a good way of explaining to my students the impact of debt. Whilst they were rationalising that there are times when debt is a fact of life, they hadn't really understood the nature of interest. This was when I told them about the cost of my house.

In the 1980s it was possible to buy a house for £26,000, as I did. I bought the house in a rather nice area near Charnwood Water in Loughborough. I stayed there for six years so it must have had something going for it and it did, it was nice and quiet with great neighbours. But back to the students. They were fine when I told them I paid about £3,000 a year in mortgage payments (bear in mind that £3,000 was worth a lot more then). When I pointed out that 25 years of £3,000 **per year** equates to £75,000 for a £26,000 debt, they were shocked. These young people learnt a very fast lesson – **borrowing money costs money** and can be every expensive.

As I write this, the figures are even more alarming. That is why I wanted to write this book, to help you understand these basic principles, and to help you get out of debt.

Now is the time for you to think and be creative. You need a pen and some paper: first of all write down all of the ways that you have incurred debt and roughly when you have borrowed in the last 12 months. Make sure you name the people or companies with whom you had a debt. This is important, these are the people who agreed to let you use their money. They made an agreement with you, that they would let you use their money for a fee. Now make a second list that includes all of the ways in which you know your friends incur debt and then add every other way you can imagine. Take the time to look at these lists – they represent the enemy. **Debt is using other people's money to buy products and services. Interest is the fee you pay to the other people for the privilege of using their money.**

So why do your lists represent the enemy? Did you notice what I said earlier? Here it is again.

This is important, these are the people who agreed to let you use their money. They made an agreement with you, that they would let you use their money **for a fee**.

They made an agreement you, they agreed to let you use their money, what did *you* agree to?

Think about this for a moment because you may find this a shock but you need to understand that they agreed to let you use their money and *you agreed to **make them wealthy**.*

Now you can be forgiven for not realising this at the time but that is exactly what you agreed to. By borrowing, you agreed that you would use other people's money and pay them a fee for doing so and that means you are paying them money to use their money. Put the shoe on the other

> You can only become truly accomplished at something you love. Don't make money your goal. Instead pursue the things you love doing, and do them so well that people can't take their eyes off you.
> Maya Angelou

foot. What if you were the one who was being paid? What if you had no debts, wouldn't that make life more fun? Imagine a world where you owned everything and didn't need to borrow, you could, via the banking system (OK, they do need to rebuild our trust after their disgraceful behaviour but go with it), lend your money for a fee. What if they were paying you? It could happen, pause for a moment and think about that, write down how it makes you feel.

Journal	In your journal write a memo for a date in the future when you predict you will be debt free. Imagine how that will feel, what will you be wearing, what colour paint will be on the walls of your home, the one you own, the one that is fully paid for and is all yours?

During the 1960s a small family businessman found his employee was lending a local man £3 a week. You have to bear in mind that at that time a working man would earn about £9 per week, so it was a sizeable amount. The employee said he always paid it back on Tuesdays. So a pattern had begun where the man borrowed it on Thursday and used it to finance his weekend drinking. He then paid it back the following week on a Tuesday and borrowed it again on a Thursday. The employee had unwittingly set himself up as a banker who was lending money for no interest. The lender had the use of the businessman's money and there was no cost involved, so from the businessman's point of view it simply did not make sense. He was losing the use of his money and was gaining no interest for doing so.

In 2007 the world economy took a nosedive and it will take years to recover. But don't worry about *the* economy, worry about *your* economy. That is what this book is about and its purpose is to debt-proof your life.

Debt-proofing your life

A debt-proof approach to living means being able to live within your means, in other words you spend less than you earn. You can give to charity and still live below your income level so that you are saving and helping others less fortunate than yourself.

Five reasons to debt proof your life

1   **To protect against hard times**. In the post-2007 world where, frankly, if it had not been for some astute leadership by certain politicians, life is going to be tougher. We woke up one morning to hear Robert Peston on the BBC tell us we had all gone broke. The idea that boom and bust were a thing of the past was fanciful nonsense. Anyone who looked at the financial system (as I did) in 2005 would have seen it was a quagmire, a real mess. We will emerge from this, but it will take time and we will all have to pay for it. Make no mistake, this will cost us all. In my view, this is the modern-day equivalent of the 1929 Wall Street Crash which led to the severe depression of the 1930s. As I write this, I have just seen a prediction that it will be 2014 before house prices revert to the level they were in 2007. That seems about right. Houses were massively over valued in the UK and it seems right that they needed to be realigned.

2   **To protect your future**. Revolving debt means you are forced to transfer your future wealth to someone else, your creditor. Remember what we said earlier, you are agreeing to make them wealthy.

3   **To reduce your stress**. You choose: you can have worry, sleepless nights, communication breakdown, depression, anxiety or you can have rest, joy, and peace of mind. Not a difficult choice is it? Money problems are a huge stress on us and our bodies bear the toll. We did hear of one young couple who were in serious debt. The young man realised he was well insured and so committed suicide one night by gassing himself with his car exhaust. He left a wife and two lovely young children without a father and they were no better off because insurance companies *do*

not pay out on suicides. This is a measure of how desperate some people can become.

4   **To avoid relationship breakdown**. Money stress is regarded as one of the main causes of relationship breakdown between couples. If you value your relationship with your partner then you owe it to them and yourself to debt-proof your life.

5   **To teach your children**. If you have children, think about the world in which they live. They have probably already read magazines with the latest must-have fashion or gadgets, watched TV and been exposed to thousands of messages designed to get them to want a product, know what a fast food so-called restaurant is like and to desire the products on sale. They have been exposed to messages that tell them they have an entitlement and to have that entitlement instantly gratified. Take a good look at your kids; are they becoming the debtors of tomorrow?

Beware of little expenses; a small leak will sink a great ship.
Benjamin Franklin

This is a little off topic but I just want to make you think about the implications of not having money.

I have said this before, but it does bear repeating: there are poor old people in the USA who are eating cat food in order to try to save enough money to pay for their medicine. That is how bad the future can be for some people and unless you like cat food you do not want to be in that situation, because as life expectancy increases, you are going to be eating cat food for a long time. These poor old people have a choice either to eat human food and go without their medication or to buy the medication and eat cat food to get enough protein in their diet. There are a reported 48 million US citizens without health insurance, one of which was a poor 13 year old boy who had an abscess. His single mother did not have health insurance and could not afford the medical bills. The abscess infected his blood stream and the boy died. He could have been treated by a 50p shot of penicillin.

The moves in certain parts of the UK, as in Wales, to make prescriptions free have been criticised by some people but when you hear stories like those above, I hope you agree the cost is worth it. I also hope you agree how important the National Health Service is in Britain and how we must protect this jewel in our crown despite what other nations may say. It must never be the case that an elderly poor British resident is forced to eat cat food on crisp bread because they cannot afford to buy both food and medication, or a child from a poor background is allowed to die because no one will fund the 50p needed to save his life.

> It has been my experience that competency in mathematics, both in numerical manipulations and in understanding its conceptual foundations, enhances a person's ability to handle the more ambiguous and qualitative relationships that dominate our day-to-day financial decision-making.
> Alan Greenspan

Impulse shopping

This is one of the easiest ways of getting into debt. My good friend Colin, on hearing I was writing this book said, 'I could do with a copy of that book, I am always impulse buying, I just do not know where the money goes'. This is why you need a spending record, which we will talk about later.

Impulse buying occurs when you see something and you just have to have it. Shops set out to make you buy something that you didn't set out to buy. Have you ever wondered why the sweets in some supermarkets are by the check-out till and are at child height? This is called pester power, they have deliberately set a trap to get your kids pestering you for sweets, so that they remove money from your pocket and put it into their tills.

There is a well known budget clothing store. When you come to pay you have to queue up in a snake-like fashion and wait for a recording vacant pay point. All along the queue area there are cheap items for sale. All you have to do is to reach out, pick them up and put them in your basket and 'Hey, what is another £5 and, after all . . .'.

I left that blank deliberately because, guess what, we all do it. By 'it' I mean we all justify the decision to spend extra. 'Well, it was only £5'. 'It was such a bargain!' 'I deserve a treat every now and again'. Every time you reach out, they have suckered you, they got you to do what they want.

Garden centres have items designed for the home at the entrance to the garden centre, and not plants or garden products. Why? The answer is simple, these are impulse buys aimed at women. Many people visit garden centres to have a day out and often aim just to visit and not buy. By putting these items on show it is an impulse buy for the purchaser.

Supermarkets always start with greengrocery by the door because it is colourful and uplifting and again we are more tempted to buy. They also pump out bakery smells at the door. The smell of newly-baked bread can make you drool, so you go in and buy some.

Have you ever wondered why supermarkets move products around? By this I mean why is it they go to the trouble of clearing, say, batteries off one shelf, carrying them to another location in the store and setting them up again? The fact is customers 'learn the store'. We learn where the products we want are situated and go to those locations. Many people then ignore other products on offer and just buy what they went in to buy. So what happens when they move products around? You need to scan the shelves to find what you usually buy and as you are scanning you see other products and so you impulse buy. They move stuff around the store to get you to see what is on offer and to impulse buy. It is more consumer heroin, it is more stuff being pushed at us to buy and it works for the supermarkets. If it didn't work, they wouldn't do it.

Don't think that it is only women who impulse buys, men do it too. I know one man who went with his son to a car auction and came home with a car for himself, a large old Jaguar, frankly a gas-guzzler. This just goes to show that men can also be caught out, it is just that we tend to buy big boys toys on impulse and that can cost.

Group impulse buying (identity or group identity)

There is another type of buying impulse, academics call this group identity. It is often the case that by buying certain products you make a statement about yourself to others. This first came home to me when I worked in a school in Somerset and a man working there said proudly, 'At half past eight on Saturday morning I was down at the supermarket to get the Harry Potter video, well you just have to have it don't you?'. Now this is not a negative comment against JK Rowling, an author whom I greatly admire, but it is a comment about the nature of marketing. By possessing the product you are part of the group. You have been branded as a consumer of a particular product.

Think about where the word 'branding' comes from. In the American wild west, cowboys used to brand cattle with hot iron bars to show who owned the cattle. Branding products is exactly the same. It is getting you to belong.

One of the most famous brands in the world is the James Bond brand. When a Bond movie is about to be released, the marketeers go into overdrive, they are brilliant at it. When *Quantum of Solace* appeared, I saw adverts in newspapers with Daniel Craig as James Bond, wearing a well-known brand of watch on his wrist. There were numerous other adverts. There was a radio programme of James Bond theme tunes, There were many items on the TV news on all channels about the forthcoming film, there were reviews on the radio. In short, it was not just a film, it was a cultural event. This creates a group identity and encourages people to buy into that identity. Men want to be like Daniel Craig who, despite being criticised when he was first appointed to the role of James Bond, has made it his own as a very masculine Bond. Women certainly find his masculine intelligence attractive. For the marketeers, James Bond in the form of the actor Daniel Craig is a joy, he is an easy concept to sell for lots of reasons including his undoubted ability to act.

So what groups are you encouraged to buy into? What about your car? Do you drive a German highly-engineered car with the well know marque on the front? What is happening here?

The truth is these brands offer a sense of values of 'identity' and we like to buy into these brands. By association we can claim to have the values of these brands. Let's look at the car again. Now don't get me wrong, German cars are superb, they are well engineered and expensive but when push comes to shove all they do is get you from one place to another. So a BMW will take you from Cardiff to London but so will a Ford Mondeo. The fact is that a Mondeo will do it far more economically, so why buy the BMW. The truth is because it makes you look smart, and maybe if you are a bloke, more attractive to women. The TV motoring journalist Jeremy Clarkson once said, 'There are three things you need to know about a car:

> How fast does it go?
> How much does it cost? and
> Does it pull? (In other words does it mean that women will be interested in me?)

Being frugal does not mean being cheap! It means being economical and avoiding waste.
Catherine Pulsifer

So are you branded by the products you buy? In *Understanding the Numbers* I talked about a woman who had a teenage daughter. The girl was very brand conscious and would not go to school in unbranded clothes, she called them 'Nicky no names'. The effect of this was that mum was working as a school minibus driver and *all* of her wages were being used to pay for branded clothes for her 13-year-old brand-conscious daughter. This is madness and it is teaching the girl how to be a debtor in the future. She is learning the price of everything but the value of nothing.

It is human nature to want it and want it now; it is also a sign of immaturity.
Dave Ramsey

3 Types of Debt: Good and Bad

In this chapter you may be surprised to find that there is actually a good type of debt. This is one of the major differences between the rich and the middle class/poor. The rich are brought up to understand that the way to get wealthy is to use your money well and where it is necessary to take on debt, make sure you incur good debt not bad debt.

Good debt and bad debt

In simple terms there are two types of debt: good debt and bad debt. Good debt is debt that you incur because it brings value back to you in the long term. Bad debt takes value away from you immediately. Rich people learn this distinction very early in their careers. The difference between the rich and the poor/middle class is how they think about money. Everyone likes a bargain but rich people buy assets, the poor and middle class buy liabilities.

Definition of an asset

An asset is something that brings money to you. In other words it goes up in value. People often use this word to mean a possession; a possession is not by definition an asset. So what are assets? They are possessions that rise in value. Some people argue that their home is their greatest asset, but I am not convinced. Yes, you have to have a home and yes, it does usually in the long term go up in value, but so does every other home. So where is the advantage? The only real advantage is that you can grow equity in your home.

So examples of assets include land, gold, art work, in fact anything that can appreciate in value, i.e. be worth more when you wish to sell it.

Definition of a liability

A liability is a purchase that takes money away from you. For instance, a car is a liability (see below) because it goes down in value. A brand new television is a liability because it goes down in value. These products take money away from you, and when you have finished using them, they are not worth as much as when you bought them.

We have to thank the US author Robert Kiyosaki for the following definition, it certainly is good, think about it;

> assets *generate money for you,*
> liabilities *take money away from you.*

Some people are very impressed by cars. They see a man or woman in an expensive car and say, 'Wow, look at how cool that is'. I don't do that any more. Cars are not an asset, cars are a liability, they go down in value. If you buy a brand new car and pay a deposit, you can pay the rest by using HP (hire purchase), so that means you have monthly outgoings that take money away from you. As soon as you drive it off the forecourt it loses a huge amount of its value. If you took a car off the forecourt, turned it around and drove it back on, it could lose as much as 40% of its value. Why? Because it is now a used car. And you still have years left to pay for it. I drive a 12-year-old Ford. In the last month I have been on two long-distance journeys in the UK and it has been fine. Cars cost money. Of course, if I applied for HP I could afford a Mercedes and would love to have one *but* I am a writer. I work from home. So very often my car is sitting on the drive all day. Why put a £30,000 car out there when a cheap but reliable one will do?

Research in America has shown quite conclusively that real millionaires do not drive fancy large cars such as a Rolls-Royce, they drive ordinary cars. Many US millionaires drive the equivalent of a Ford Mondeo or a Vauxhall Astra. The reason they do this is quite simple, they recognise that the purpose of the car is to get you from a to b. They do not need to impress anyone and so do not set out to do so. There is one exception to this and that is people who do a lot of mileage. If you are driving over 500 miles per week as part of your job then a quality car is an essential purchase not a luxury. However, do not assume that a company car is the best way to do this. Talk to an accountant and minimise your tax liability (people who are allocated company cars in the UK face a tax liability, so it might be better for you to provide the car yourself and charge the company a mileage charge, Her Majesty's Revenue & Customs (HMRC) do allow such a system).

Bad or stupid debt

HOLDEN MAN

Whilst we are talking about cars I want to tell you about Holden man. A Holden is a very good Australian family car. On a British TV documentary I saw a man who had imported a Holden from Australia to the UK. Now my Aussie friends, please don't be offended when I say this, but a Holden is not really in the list of most desirable cars. Be honest, it isn't like a Rolls-Royce or a Ferrari or Mercedes, it is a Holden. So what did our Holden man do? He started to make it smarter. He started to customise it. According to the TV documentary he spent £55,000 on this car. Every gadget, every gizmo you can think of went into the car. Cool huh? No, really silly. The reason this was silly was because to pay for this customisation, he had to borrow the money. Did he go to the bank? No. He took out the equity on his home. The equity on a house is the increase in value from the price you paid for it. So, say you bought your house for £175,000 and it is now worth £200,000, it means you have £25,000 in the house. However, if you remortgage and spend it on a liability (remember cars are liabilities) you now have a mortgage of £200,000. The money you have spent on the car is someone else's money and will take 25 years to pay back. *Twenty-five years.*

What will the value of that Holden be in 25 years' time? It may go up in value but it will probably have been scrapped a long time ago and be worth a lot less – only the scrap value. In the UK today it is possible to buy a very good used car for less than £10,000. So for that money he could have bought at least five cars. Assuming he runs them for an average of seven years each, that is 35 years of motoring. This was not the brightest of things to do with his money. Now if he had £55,000 that he didn't need to borrow, well fine, enjoy my friend, enjoy, but in reality he spent the kids' inheritance.

This is not the first time I have seen this sort of silly thinking. Years ago, when I was a maths teacher Leicester, I was at a meeting with other maths teachers when, as blokes do, we were talking about cars. This guy then piped up, 'I have found a brilliant cheap way of buying a brand new car.' Immediately he had our interest. 'OK', I said as the other six men were also intrigued and were silently urging him to explain more. He beamed the ultimate smile of the foolish and said 'Put it on your mortgage, it only costs £28 per month'. This was during the 1980s when it was possible to buy a new car for a few thousand pounds, so let's do some basic maths.

$$£28 \text{ per month for 25 years} = £8,400$$

This car would be a heap of scrap by the time he had finished paying for it and it would have cost him three times what he would have paid if he had taken out a conventional loan. Remember, this guy was a maths teacher. Are you surprised that the mortgage company lent him the money? Also remember their job is to make money for their shareholders, so they got back £300 for every £100 they lent him, which is good business for them.

Recognising the difference between good and bad debt

It is important to recognise the difference between good debt and bad debt. Bad debt is debt where you buy liabilities – these are products that go down in value. Good debt is debt where you buy you buy assets – these are products that go up in value.

Remember, assets bring money to you, liabilities take money from you. In my view borrowing a lot of money to have a flash car is a bad debt in most cases. Why do I say most cases and not all cases? Well, as I have said above, if you have a job where you are on the road every day and use your car as an office, then it means your car is earning money for you, so in this case it becomes an investment, an office on wheels. Remember, it is still losing money, it still goes down in value, but instead of paying for a bricks and mortar office, this is your office so in that case it makes good sense to have the best quality, reliable car you can afford.

What about your home?

This is not easy to define. Some finance writers argue that this is a liability in that it takes money from you. But it is not that simple. You have to have somewhere to live and on average in the UK house prices double every seven years. So in about seven years the house you live in will probably be worth twice what it is worth now. This is where it can go wrong for some people. In seven years the house price has doubled, so say it cost you £175,000, it will now be worth £350,000. So there is value in it of £175,000 *but* don't think this is easy money to spend, it isn't.

We heard of a woman who had taken the money from her home and bought lots of (you guessed it), liabilities. She had doubled her mortgage from £70,000 to £140,000. This is very silly. She went out and bought a dingy and toys for the children and holidays on what she called 'free money'. It is *not* free; she will spend the rest of her mortgage period paying for them and, they will have gone down in value.

Financially-savvy people do something similar, they take equity from their home and go shopping *but* the difference is they buy assets. In this book I do not intend to write a lot about property because we plan to look at property later in this series, but it is worth a brief comment.

In 2005 in the first book in this series I predicted the credit crunch (but not the sub-prime scandal in the USA). It was obvious that we couldn't carry on and the new US President will not be able to do anything about this, because it is a global crisis. However, in times like this, the rich can get richer and the poor will probably get poorer. Is property still a good bet? Yes is the answer but only if you do your homework.

First of all, in the UK (and if you are reading this in another country I'm afraid I cannot comment on the property situation in your country) there is a shortage of homes. This means the fundamentals of the market are there, in other words there is a demand. However, there are dangers in the market. There have been too many so-called 'property clubs' that have encouraged members to buy into the illusion of city-centre apartment living. This has meant there has been an over-supply of apartments (or flats as we call them in the UK). It means that many investors have paid far too much for flats that cannot be rented out. So there are opportunities here because there are a number of distressed landlords who want to sell. So would I recommend investing in flats? Well, in London yes, but elsewhere, no. In London there is a shortage of property, so there is demand. In other words if you were to have a flat for rent in London you would have a good chance in getting a tenant. But outside of London I am not convinced. We are not a flat-living culture. Britons like living in houses with gardens, so this seems to me to be a better bet, but you must make your own decision. A word of warning, calculate the mean (average) rental yield in the area you are considering buying in and make sure you get it right. If the rental yield is not at least 130% of the mortgage payment do not touch it. This is the minimum I would recommend.

So in general, although some say a home is a liability in that it costs you money, I would argue that on the basis that you need somewhere to live, it makes sense to buy proportionately to your income.

> **CASE STUDY**
> **We know of one young man who rents a flat in a city centre apartment block with another person. He is paying a four-figure rent a year for half the rent of the flat. He could buy a small terraced house for less than this price. But the young man is 'living the lifestyle'. He believes he is entitled to a city-centre lifestyle, but has not earned it (he has dropped out of university to do this). This is foolish. He is living a lifestyle he simply cannot sustain.**

Revolving credit cards

Yes, we did this as well but it is not sustainable. Revolving credit cards means maxing out on 0% cards and then when the free period is over, swapping the debt to another card. This does not pay off the debt it simply moves it around. Not a practice to be recommended unless you really know what you are doing. We did hear of one buyer who bought a Jaguar car on 0% credit with a card (this may be an urban myth). He revolved the cards for three years and then sold the Jag for £3,000 less than he paid for it. Smart move – as long as he has the £3,000 to pay it off. This is called being a 'card tart' but you must keep on the ball, otherwise if you are hit for interest payments it will hurt. It is not a strategy I recommend personally. It's your decision.

Financial freedom requires not just insights but also actions, and to carry out these actions you must learn about money and how it needs to be treated.
Suze Orman

Silly daily debt

We call this silly daily debt because that is exactly what it is. It is debt you incur daily because, and no disrespect meant to you, it is easier to spend that to do something. For instance, isn't it easier to pop out to the supermarket and buy a sandwich rather than make one at home? Well, we don't think so. Look at the time element, it takes less than ten minutes to make a sandwich, about the same time a lot of people take to leave the office and buy one. So you don't save time.

Sandwiches in the UK are not cheap. You may be surprised if you are reading this in other countries but it can cost around £5 for a ham roll in some areas (approximately $10) and then there is the coffee that you really do have to have. Before you write in, we have checked this and at the time of writing these figures are accurate and not an exaggeration. We found sandwiches and rolls ranging from £1.75 per sandwich to £5.70 and this was not in London. Many vendors sell coffee to tube travellers and train travellers, again this is not cheap. We have seen prices of £2.75 for a cup of coffee and we suspect there are far higher prices. OK do the mathematics.

Say you spend £2.50 per day on sandwiches that comes to 5 × 2.50 = £12.50 per week.

Say you have four weeks' holiday per year this comes to 48 × £12.50 = £600 (and we have not even had coffee yet).

Add £1.50 per day for coffee, so that is 5 × £1.50 × 48 = £360.

Total it and we get £960 per year.

So at a guess this means you work about four weeks per year just to pay for the lunch you buy. Now does it look so good?

A loaf of bread costs about £1 and will last one week. Say you spent £5 on sandwich filler and a one-off £5 for a thermos flask. A jar of coffee, say £3, that lasts say three weeks, now do the mathematics.

48 loaves of bread	£48
16 jars of coffee at £3 each	£48
1 thermos flask	£5
48 lots of sandwich filler at £5 per week	£240
Total	£341

Amount saved: £960 − £341 = **£619**

That is £619 in your pocket and you have not missed out on lunch, in fact you could probably have had a better lunch. The only downside is carrying the flask and sandwich to work but you are saving big time. £600+ per year will buy a lot of new clothes or pay for an extra holiday, or pay off some debt that you have and you don't need to work overtime to get them, all from making your own sandwiches. Just a thought but a good one isn't it!

> Start saving right now, and don't stop until you die.
> Ben Stein

SMOKING AND THE CARIBBEAN

I confess, for a short time when I was young, I did smoke. I smoked cigars because I liked them. When I was teaching in a school in Wales I lit up in the staffroom (it was not illegal then) and coughed like crazy. I then said to someone 'I shall have to give these up or I'll look like Bob when I am 50.' I was shocked to hear Bob was only 32 years old. I put the cigar out and threw him the pack. I am now near 50 and Bob is dead.

> Success in money terms means being solvent. If you approach life by trying to keep up with the Joneses you are not thinking right. Success in life means being secure that is what money gives you; life is not an Ipod for an Ipod.
> Dr Graham Lawler aka Mr Educator

If you smoke, you really must give up, if not for your health, then for your pocket. Look at the mathematics.

1 packet of cigarettes costs about £5 at the time of writing. Say you smoke 20 per day this is 7 packs per week, at a cost of £35 per week.

There are 52 weeks in the year so £35 × 52 = £1,820

This is how much money you are literally burning in a year.
What is the link with the Caribbean? Well, on the day we
checked it was possible to go to the Caribbean for a week's
holiday for less than this amount. So by cutting out
smoking you could go to the Caribbean every year for the
rest of your life based on what you are spending on
cigarettes now. You are simply re-routing the money you
spend (and doing great things for your health).

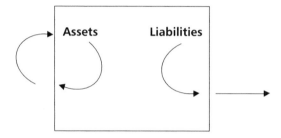

As mentioned above, the American writer Robert Kiyosaki
puts it well, he says 'Assets feed you, liabilities eat you'.
Assets bring money to you; liabilities take money away from
you. Look at what happens when you buy assets, you set up
a circular motion. Assets generate cash that comes back to
you but liabilities take cash away from you.

Don't confuse assets with possessions, just because you own
something does not make it an asset. When I lived in
Somerset I served on a parish council for a short time. They
had a multi-user games area (MUGA) in the village. Now I
have written about this before because it is such a good
example of how a poor understanding of mathematics leads
to stupidity. A well-known local councillor pushed for this
and was part of a group who organised a questionnaire to
seek support. As a former mathematics teacher I pointed
out that the questionnaire was biased, it led people to give
the answers the people who developed the questionnaire
wanted. When I pointed this out to the lady concerned she
agreed that it could have been better worded but the

questionnaire went out. The response from the village was 9.5%, over 90% of the village did not respond. Of the 9.5% who did respond, the majority were in favour, but this is hardly surprising. In fact of the 9.5% who did respond, 98% were in favour *but* this was 98% of the 9.5% respondents *not* 98% of those who were polled. But confusion reigned and as a consequence the MUGA went ahead. This was meant to create income for the village and as such be an asset but surprise, surprise, it actually lost money, so imagine my amazement when I heard the village clerk refer to this as an asset. Remember what Kiyosaki said, 'Assets feed you, liabilities eat you', assets bring money to you, liabilities take money from you. You decide what the MUGA was, I know what my view is.

4　Debt Traps

When I was a boy we had a pet dog. He was a corgi and he was beautiful. When we had him, I was about eight years old and he came a small pup with folded back ears. The next step was what to call him. As children we had just been taken to see *Bambi* and my brother thought the dog looked like Thumper the rabbit in *Bambi* so we called him Thumper. Now as dogs go, corgis are smart little dogs. They are the Queen's favourite dog and they originally came from Wales. They were popular with cattle drovers in years gone by for driving cattle to London. These little dogs could nip the back heels of cattle to drive them on yet because they were so low to the ground they could escape the inevitable kick of the beast as it sought to remove this nuisance from its heels. (*Ci* is Welsh for dog and *cor* was a type of cowshed used on many Welsh farms so *Cor Ci* or cowshed dog, over time became corgi.) Now Thumper was one smart cookie, he loved being part of the family but he had a will of his own, especially when it came to swallowing worm tablets. This was something he just was not prepared to do. So picture the scene, here we are throwing pills into the back of Thumper's mouth and he, quite happily spits them out again.

Dad was a butcher who ran his own business. Dad also knew a thing or two about dogs and took the worming pill and wrapped it into a small morsel of meat. He then offered the same pill to Thumper wrapped up in a nice tasty piece of meat and Thumper swallowed it every time. Debt is like Thumper's worming pill, when it is wrapped up in a nice juicy morsel it can become irresistible and we've just got to take a bite. That is how we are encouraged to get into debt.

Recently I saw an advert for a car supermarket. It said you need pay nothing for five months and you can drive away with your car today. This is the debt equivalent of Thumper's worming pill. I may not have to pay anything for five months but as sure as anything I will have to pay.

Thumper didn't link the rather unpleasant effect of his worming tablet with the meat he had eaten but you can link the unpleasant effect of the debt that you have taken out. In the same way Thumper was conned, we can all be conned and we all know how restricting those traps that are set can be.

> The safe way to double your money is to fold it over once and put it in your pocket.
> Frank Hubbard

Be clear in your own mind: retailers, advertisers and big businesses all want you to spend, they all want you to take on debt because that is what makes them money. Think about it, by setting debt traps for us, they make money and that is why they do it. All of the adverts, all of the sales messages you see in one day are designed to get you to exchange your money for goods.

Types of debt trap

Credit card accounts

These are great if they are managed correctly. One of the easiest ways we are persuaded to use credit cards is by the pre-approved application. This is a great boost to the ego. You have been pre-approved, yes, little old you out of the millions of people on the planet – they have chosen you. But you will pay for it. I remember getting one of these and it said something along the lines of 'You are now at the stage in your career where success brings its own problems. Fortunately you have been pre-approved for the *******
card. All you need to do is sign and return this form.'
Phew, how lucky was that! Here I was, a very successful person (they said so, so it must be true) and that brought problems with it (they said that as well, so again it must be true) but fortunately they had the answer, their credit card. Well, wasn't I the lucky one? Did you see the pattern? Exemplify a problem and provide the solution. This is an old sales technique. What they do is tell you there is a problem and then tell you that they can sell you the solution – lucky that, isn't it?

It is essential to know what you have spent and when and where you have spent it. We will look at tools to do this later but in the meantime I am going to suggest that you *do need* credit cards. This is at odds with most financial gurus but times are changing. Most experts suggest that it is only by living a cash only life that you can get out of debt but the fact is in the twenty-first century there are many places which will *not* accept cash or cheques. It is a sad fact that there are counterfeit coins and notes in circulation and therefore the only way to buy many products is to have a credit card. I recommend two cards for personal use, one as a backup if the first is refused *but* you must pay if off to the penny every month (see Chapter 5 for more details). If you run a business you may need more. For instance, we have one card which is solely dedicated to buying fuel for the business. We buy nothing else on this credit card except fuel. This helps keep the management of the accounts simple. In a similar way we have a separate account that is for stationery. Again it is very easy to manage.

This only works, however, when it is managed properly on a daily, weekly and monthly basis. Please do always keep in mind that a lot of debt is dangerous, especially for people on low income and students. When you have debt problems it can cause anxiety, remorse, depression and an inability to concentrate. In cases like this, debt has control of you and you need to reassert yourself and become its master. As I said in *Understanding the Numbers*, the first book in this short series, *'banks are your enemy'*. Sear that on your soul dear reader for verily it is true.

The purpose of a bank is to make money for its owners, the shareholders. They do it by lending money and charging a fee for lending that money. Their objective is to take money out of your pocket and out it into their collective pocket. The credit crunch that started in late 2007 has changed nothing except to say it is now harder to get credit. They still aim to make money out of you, if you will let them.

Do not use credit cards to buy things you cannot afford. Do remember that if you are patient you will be able, eventually, to have everything you want but not have to go into debt for it.

Every time you incur debt, you are using someone else's money and it will need to be paid back. Not only will the money need to be paid back but you will also need to pay a fee for using someone else's money, that fee is called interest. Remember the purpose of this book is to educate you in financial intelligence. We want to help you clear debt so we are looking at ways of cutting back and paying off debt. Investments will come later, when you are debt free.

The annual percentage rate (APR)

APR is important, it is a measure of the fee you are paying. The annual percentage rate describes the interest rate for a whole year, rather than just a monthly fee or rate. This fee is across the whole year and so is called 'annualised'.

There is also another measure called 'the effective APR'. Now let's just think about this for a moment: If you borrow £100 for a year, in the first month you will incur interest payments, this is the fee for borrowing the money. It depends on how the loan is structured, but it is possible that you could start paying interest on the interest of the loan, this is why the effective APR is so important. The effective APR has been called the mathematically true interest rate. The point to remember is that you may find you are paying interest on the interest and this is far more common than you may realise.

In real terms, we have found some store cards are horrendous ways of borrowing. In the UK some store cards have almost 30% APR. This means that when you buy, say, clothes from a well-known high street store costing £100, in fact they are costing you £130. You are paying a £30 fee for the privilege of using someone else's money, that is how expensive these cards can be.

In the UK and the USA lenders are required by law to disclose the APR before the loan (or credit application) is completed. However, the definition of APR is not the same in both countries. The APR in the UK and Europe often looks higher than the equivalent US rate. This is because the UK/EU rate is the effective rate whilst the US rate is the nominal rate. You need to know the effective rate. Can you see now why it is so important that we change the culture of lending and live within our means? The alternative is a lifetime of debt.

The credit crunch that started in 2007 is a warning. We have been living beyond our means for far too long and now we must pay back what we have borrowed.

Monthly instalment plans

These are designed to get money out of your pocket and into their pocket. Are you seeing a pattern yet? They make payments easier for you. In fact you only need to pay a small amount every month. But look at it another way, every pound you have is building wealth. The question is: whose wealth are you building? By using monthly payment plans you are building up the wealth of your creditors. Can you see what they are doing? By providing monthly plans they are getting you to overspend and use credit. Credit is compound interest that works for the creditor, not for you unless you are the one doing the lending or saving.

I drive an old car, it is reliable but I am starting to think that I will need to replace it in about a year. So will I get a monthly plan to pay a deposit and then put the rest down, no way! Well actually I already have a monthly plan but for me not the creditor. You see I think that I will need to replace my car in about 12 to 18 months so I am now paying myself a monthly fee to save for the car. All things being equal, this means I get the car when I need it, I have a monthly plan to pay for it and the compound interest comes to *me* because I have invested the monthly payments in a savings account that means I get interest on the interest.

When it comes to buying a replacement car, I will not be buying a brand new car but a good used model. Why? The answer is simple: it is because a new car depreciates incredibly quickly. It loses 25% of its value when you drive it off the forecourt because it is not new any more. So instead of a 60-month payment plan, I have a savings plan in place instead. Instead of paying the car finance company I pay me. And when it comes to buying a replacement car, I bargain hard. At the time of writing there is a glut of cars in the UK. They cannot shift new cars so second-hand or used cars are at an all-time low. This means that they are going to be grateful to shift stock off the forecourt, so don't be afraid to haggle. We know of cases where brand new cars have been discounted by over £10,000 just to get the car sold so it should be easy to get a few thousand off a used car. Have a look on Ebay. Many sellers of cars are actually garages and they do sell with a warranty so it is not as risky as it might appear. Don't forget to ask for flaps and mats (mudguards and car mats) and what about a tow bar as well?

Overdrafts

Again, this is using other people's money and again you are making the lender wealthier. Sometimes you may have little choice but to use an overdraft, but it will cost you.

Taxes

You have no choice, you must pay your taxes *but* you do not need to buy things and pay the taxes on them. In the

UK there is a tax called VAT (value added tax). It is usually 17.5% – although in 2009 the government made a temporary reduction to 15% to try to increase spending. So every time you buy a product which is subject to VAT, you are paying tax, so ask yourself – do you *really* need it?

Do not be tempted to evade income tax, it is illegal and HMRC takes a dim view of tax evasion. We have heard many horror stories of people who thought they were smarter than the taxman – they were not. One businessman is said to have travelled to Spain for ten days of work and claimed for them against his tax. He took his wife (she worked for the company so that was quite legitimate), but he stayed for five days' holiday and claimed that against tax – big mistake. The story goes that the taxman took notice of his trip and the fact that he illegally claimed for the five days of holiday. He ended up on a holiday at Her Majesty's pleasure, ten months in prison.

Student loans

Check out the details and make sure you understand them. There is a great website (www.slc.co.uk) with details from the Student Loan Company. Also look at www.studentloanrepayment.co.uk. At the time of writing the interest rate on the loan has just been reduced but you do need to check and ensure that you are up to date. If you fall behind, do contact them and discuss your difficulties, you cannot walk away from these debts. It is a burden but you should find that as an investment, your education will be invaluable. There are different contact details depending on where you live in the UK so ensure that you are contacting the right area. In Wales there is a Welsh version available.

At the time of writing the repayment is made through the tax system and only begins after the student has left higher education and is earning a certain amount. The loans accrue interest at the rate of inflation, which is a very good deal since it means the amount repaid has the same value as the amount borrowed.

Dental bills

NHS dentists are rare to find but they are available. If you do need to go private you will pay. Try googling dentists + NHS + your area and you should find someone. The cost of private dental care is often a vanity, something that can be bragged about in the golf club. As an aspiring wealthy person you know that real wealth is what you have in your bank account, not what you spend.

Personal loans

Personal loans are a debt. I have had them and had to pay back far more than I borrowed. If it is an emergency then you have little choice, but think about it this way, do you really need it? I used a personal loan to buy the first five cars I owned. Now look at the pattern here. I would go to the bank and ask for a loan. I would then buy a three- to five-year-old car and pay off the loan. So the loan took about two to three years to pay and guess what, by then the car was old and unreliable so I had little choice but to repeat the pattern. For car number six, which I still have, we did things differently we saved the money first. I didn't need to borrow, I went to the car showroom, told them what I wanted and managed to get a substantial discount for paying cash. It really does work.

Nigeria 419

In a post-2007 world where money is very tight for everyone, it is very easy to fall prey to unscrupulous people. Imagine the scene – you log onto the internet one morning with worries swirling around your head. The children need new shoes, the mortgage is due and the car needs a new exhaust and you do not know where the money is coming from – and then an email arrives offering you $10 million.

Do you remember that old saying, 'If it looks too good to be true, it generally is too good to be true'? This is one of those cases. The people who send these emails are fraudsters who are trying to *take money away from you*. During the preparation of this book we received a number of this type of email. If they had all been true, I would now have over $250,000,000 in my bank account but I do not, because they come from dishonest people. The following are just some of the frauds that are being perpetrated and this is not an exhaustive list.

I am going to devote quite a bit of space to this because it is an increasingly common scam that can lead you into a huge amount of debt. The 419 scam is a confidence trick where a target, also known as 'the mark', is persuaded to advance sums of money in the hope of getting a larger gain. Usually they are promised a significantly larger gain and it is usually millions of pounds or dollars. This scam originated in Nigeria in the early 1980s when the oil-based economy was in decline. The 419 refers to refers to the article of the Nigerian Code (part of Chapter 38 'Obtaining property by false pretences; Cheating') dealing with fraud. It needs to be said that the Nigerian authorities are aware of this and that there are many decent hard-working Nigerian businesses who are tainted by these criminals, but it is a widespread scam and it works. It is called an advanced fee fraud and is similar to the older Spanish prisoner fraud. In the Spanish prisoner fraud a target would be told that if he sends money (to be used to bribe guards) then the rich prisoner will show his gratitude later, obviously this never happens.

The Nigerian 419 scam usually starts with an email which is supposedly sent to a selected recipient but is in fact sent to many people and makes an offer that will result in the recipient being paid a large amount of money. There are variations on the story, but usually it is a person who knows of the existence of a large amount of money that he cannot access directly because he has no right to it. The recipient is offered a huge amount of money in return for their help, often tens of millions of dollars. The majority of recipients ignore such emails, (in fact as I write this in the Aber Publishing offices this morning we have had two such emails) but a small proportion of people do reply and that is what makes them so lucrative for the thieves. Although these scams are known as 419, don't be fooled into thinking these scammers operate only from Nigeria, they operate from every continent.

The next step for the scammer is to develop a relationship with you where they ask for small sums of money, say $1,000 to pay for a local tax or a bribe. The person being duped will then hand this over and see it as an investment since they hope to get millions of dollars back in return. The victim has not yet realised he is having his money stolen. Variations on the scam include a relative of a deposed African leader who amassed a stolen fortune, a wealthy foreigner who deposited millions in the country before dying unexpectedly, usually in a car or air crash leaving no will and no family, and a relatively new scam is the US soldier. In this version the soldier has accidentally stumbled across a hidden fortune in Iraq, usually a cache of gold. The money from these scams is said by the thief to be in the form of gold bullion, gold dust, millions of dollars actually in an account, blood diamonds (diamonds in a war zone that are sold to finance an insurgency or other act of warfare) or a series of other banking formats like cheques or bank drafts.

The scammers will often send official looking documents but there are often clues that give them away. For instance they will be using an email account for a provider like hotmail or Yahoo or gmail. Very often the phone number will be a mobile number, hardly the way an official would work in any country.

Once contact has been made, a hurdle will be put in place. This will be a delay or a monetary hurdle that prevents the deal going as planned and they will ask the target to send some money. A reason is always given, like bribing an official or paying a local tax. This is then followed by a number of other hurdles but at all times the promise of vast amounts of money is kept alive, this is to convince the target that their investment will be worthwhile since the vast wealth they believe wrongly that they will obtain, will be worth it. Sometimes the scammer will apply psychological pressure by suggesting that they have had to sell everything and since they live in a poor African village they are struggling yet you in the West have everything. Again this is all lies.

There is some evidence to suggest that a few people do actually 'run' multiple personas on line and are responsible for many of the crimes being committed. They work in offices and are professionally organised and often have contacts in the government. If the target tries to research the background of the offer it will often fit together extremely well and be very convincing. But please remember the essential fact of an advance fee fraud is that the payment to the target never happens, the gold or the gold dust or whatever does not exist. The scammers rely on the fact that by the time the victim realises he has been duped; the money (often tens of thousands of pounds or dollars) has been sent and is untraceable. In case you think this is not something that could happen in the UK we know of one couple who handed over £30,000 before they realised they were being conned.

There is one version of the scam where the thief claims to have legitimate contacts for legitimate business loan. The victim does not believe anything illegal is going on. The fraudster will meet and act as a broker asking for payment in advance, a normal practice. When the loan does not materialise the victim may be left thinking that this was down to bad luck in business and not realise he had been conned.

The thieves often send their emails from internet cafes who close their doors overnight so the scammers can work from 7 pm until the following morning. We have seen suggestions that only one in 12 million of these scams are carried out. But look at the figures, if one scammer gets one victim per 12 million emails and sends out 48 million in one night (entirely possible) then he will get four victims per night. We know of victims who have been conned out of £30,000, so say each victim is worth £20,000, that makes £80,000 per night, seven nights per week, or more than half a million pounds per week.

Victims are often asked to submit bank account details, this can be a test to judge the gullibility of the victim. They will almost always ask for the money to be wire transferred stating this is the fastest way to get the lump sum to the victim. The real reason is that wire transfers are irreversible and untraceable. According to some Internet sources, fraudsters also employ 'heavies' or men that threaten reprisals if the victim tries to leave the deal. There are cases on record of Westerners who, having been conned, have gone to Nigeria to try to retrieve their money. These people have then been murdered. The people engaged in these cons are *not* nice people, you really do not want to be part of it.

The job

This is another version of the scam where you are asked to work for the scamster in what appears to be a legal job. Your job is to take money orders, process them and take 10% for the task. The cheques sent to you are counterfeit. The banking system can take up to one month to clear foreign cheques so in the meantime the bank 'floats' your payment. This is until the cheque clears from the foreign bank. When the bank finds the cheque has bounced they want their money back and you are the person to whom they will turn. So a $4,000 cheque lands on your doorstep, you cash it in good faith and then hey presto the bank will want $3,600 back from you because they will have paid it to the foreign bank ($400 having been deducted for your fee).

The reference

We have had a newer version if the scam where the initial contact is from a woman supposedly in the USA. She tells how she has benefited by tens of millions of dollars and that when they get in touch they are genuine. This is called the softening-up phase. It is designed to make you more likely to agree to the scam. Well after all, if she is involved and has benefited, why shouldn't you? The only problem is she does not really exist and the email supposedly from her is part of the scam.

The wedding and the time share

This is another variation on the scam. The time-share owner is approached and offered an amazing rent well above the normal rent for the time due to the fact that it is a special occasion, usually a wedding. Then the event has to be called off due to something like a death in the family. The booker will ask for most of his money to be wire transferred back and ask you to keep a small but generous amount and guess what, when the cheque clears there will be no funds and the bank will once again come to you for their money.

The hitman

We received one of these in 2007 and it was scary. The hitman said that he had a contract out on one of us and we were not to go to the police, we did. The police took it seriously and it was they who told us it was a version of this scam. The hitman says that for a fee he will reverse the hit and kill the person who ordered the hit on you. If you do get one of these emails then first of all do not panic. The give-away details are that it usually will come from an online email provider, like hotmail or gmail or Yahoo. Secondly, despite what it says about contacting the police, make that 999 call. There is a purpose here, first of all it ensures that this is recorded and as such it is a crime. The sender has made a threat against your person and is therefore guilty of a crime. In reality he has probably sent 12 million threats overnight from Nigeria and if the sender gets one response, he has made a handsome profit for his night's work.

Secondly, if you have been involved in anything suspect, make sure you tell all to the police. We had to account for ourselves in terms of who we met and did business with and only then were they satisfied that this was a genuine con. In Britain today there are gangsters who are unpleasant people and who do issue contracts on others, and sometimes these contracts have been carried out on innocent victims who are mistaken for the real target, so do make that call.

There are other variations including a lottery scam, so you have been warned. According to Special Agent James Caldwell of the United States Secret Service Financial Crimes Division, in 1996–7 in the USA alone, at least $100 million was conned from the public. Now more than ten years on we think that can at least be tripled on a worldwide basis, so that at least $300 million dollars per year is being conned from people. In the UK in 2006 at least £150 million was conned out of people. Many people do not report the crime due to feeling foolish at being caught out.

Scam baiting

There are a number of websites that actively bait the scammers and waste their time. Whilst we can understand the desire to get even, make no mistake these people are ruthless thugs and probably murderers. We did see a site by 'Miss Young' who we think is doing a great job and indeed www.419eater.com is a great site *but* our advice is to avoid these guys. They are not nice people. If you do answer them **do not** give them any real information like your real ID or a real address, they can come knocking at your door. Like we said above, our advice is to avoid these guys.

Planning to be Debt Free

Surrender, stop denying. It is time, certainly by this chapter, to surrender to the fact that you have overspent. I did, most of us do and it can be a painful lesson to have to readjust but the fact is no one else can do it for you, you have to. So surrender to the fact that whilst in the past you may have been foolish with money, the future is going to be different.

The future *is* going to be different, *you* are now in charge not the credit card company. The letters from the credit card companies are a temptation, but do not be tempted. You must have seen them, I get them quite often and I have a wonderful revenge trick that I learnt from an American author. In the unsolicited letter there is a form for you to sign and return, **do not sign it**. Cut it up and put it back into the envelope. Across your name write 'No thanks' and put it in the prepaid envelope. Send that little piece of credit heroin back to them, you don't need it. You are becoming financially clean.

To bankrupt or not bankrupt that is the question

This depends on the amount of debt you have. (I can only talk about England and Wales here, if you live elsewhere you will need to check the facts under your own law.)

What about bankruptcy or an independent involuntary arrangement (IVA)?

Bankruptcy

Bankruptcy is, in my view, a last resort. When you are made bankrupt you are freed from overwhelming debt in order to make a fresh start but there are some restrictions.

Anyone can go bankrupt, including individual members who are in a partnership. However if you do become bankrupt there are implications.

- You lose control of your assets. This means someone else tells you what you can and cannot do with your money.

Look at what happens:

- You cannot get credit above a low limit to buy things (but when you have finished this programme you will not need it).

- You cannot act as a company director.

- You can only be involved in running a limited company with the permission of the court.

- You cannot trade in any business unless you tell all concerned about the bankruptcy.

- You cannot be a chartered accountant, a lawyer or a Justice of the Peace.

- You cannot be an MP or member of a local authority.

- Your credit can be affected for years to come (this does have an impact on, say, your ability to buy a home).

- You may have to endure public examination in court.

You can also expect to have your situation mentioned in the local press where you live and in the *London Gazette*. You will also have a mountain of forms to fill in, have any business you own immediately closed down, lose assets like your house and any pension you may have, have people like the building society and any creditors immediately informed. As well as this, all bank accounts, credit cards etc are closed and anything on lease or hire purchase, such as your car, will be immediately returned. We haven't really touched on how much professional, business and personal status you would lose, so what about an IVA?

Individual involuntary arrangement

An IVA is an individual voluntary arrangement where a
legal contract is drawn up between you and your creditors.
The aim is to reach a compromise between you and your
creditors, to avoid the possibility of bankruptcy. It allows
you to pay off your debt over a period of usually three to
five years. The benefit of an IVA is that it is private. After
the period of payment the remaining debt is wiped off
leaving you debt free. Again this is something you really
want to avoid. Why?

In our view both bankruptcy and IVAs need to be a last
resort because it won't change your underlying spending
pattern, your underlying psychology of spending. To do that
you need to understand how money makes you feel.

Journal
How does spending make you feel? Write down a series of
single words that says exactly how you feel when you buy
things?
Here are a few suggestions: happy, excited, thrilled, scared,
nervous. Now you think of some.

In your journal write a letter to yourself explaining how it
makes you feel. Here is my letter to me:

Dear Graham
   *I went to town today with no particular purpose in mind
but the shops had a sale and so I just had to buy
something. Now you know I have a thing about books,
maybe that is why I became a writer but hey that is another
story. Well, you will never guess what, one of the Dragons
from the TV show has a new book out and the book just
looked so great I knew I had to have it. So I bought it and it
was only £18.99 but it is such a great investment, I sure am
lucky to get it.*

Regards
Graham

Now write back and point out the stupidity of this behaviour.

Dear Graham

   So you went to town, I guess you must have been bored, but why didn't you do something else with your time, instead of driving into town and getting into debt? OK I know you like books but did you really need to buy this one? Why didn't you try the town library where you could have borrowed it for free? You say it was an investment, but who for? The Dragon you mentioned is already very rich and you just gave him more money, not the brightest of days for you, was it?

Graham

The purpose of these letters is to show how you have changed. We all change as we go through life and this programme is about helping you to change from a debtor into a saver. Then when you are a saver:

1   you contribute to the wealth of the country as a whole because your savings are used to invest in industry, etc;

2   you are demonstrating that you are a superior person because the mark of a superior mind is deferred gratification (putting off having it now in order to have more later); and

3   you are building a pot of loot to invest to make money for yourself.

Remember the big thing is to take one day at a time, so as I have already said: today you are not going to add to your debt.

Don't buy sandwiches and a coffee from a well known store, instead take sandwiches and a flask to work today, and look at what you saved, easily £5. Here is a scary piece of mathematics, £5 per day, five days per week, 48 weeks per year is how much?

It is £1,200 Wouldn't that go a long way to paying off your debt? If you are reading this in London or another big city you may find that £5 per day is actually too low. Look at it another way, that is £1,200 per year for 40 working years and that my friend (ignoring inflation) is £48,000 and all you have had is a sandwich and a coffee. That £48,000 would pay a huge amount off your mortgage or be a great investment for your retirement. That is the true cost of your sandwich. (Actually it isn't. There is also the cost of what that £48,000 could have earned had it been invested, but that is another story.)

There is a purpose in this programme, pay down debt, invest money and then you can be wealthy and then my friend you can have it all and my fervent wish is for you to have it all.

Why do I have debt?

The simple answer is we live in a culture of debt. The banks, the high street stores, the credit card companies are all in it together. They are all in the game of giving us credit because it suits them to do so. The best kind of customer they can have is someone who does *not* pay their credit card bill. Why? The answer is because he or she will need to make payments to them forever. They will be earning interest on the interest payments. Like I have said before, who do you think pays for their office tower blocks and their fancy homes. You and I do that is who, when we use credit. Well, excuse me for being smug, but I don't any more. I am happy to say that we have no personal debt other than a mortgage and we are making strides to clear that one as fast as possible. The culture of keeping you in debt, of selling you stuff to clutter your home is one that suits the creditors and not you. It keeps revenue streams rolling to them and not you, that is why you have to change.

How do I know if I am credit dependent?

Being credit dependent does not happen overnight, it is something we are brought up to expect. These days in schools students are taught how to use a credit card (didn't happen in my day as I have said elsewhere). In other words, there is an expectation that you must have a credit card because, well how else would you survive? Can you see what is happening here? Instead of being brought up with an expectation that young people will live within their means they are immediately being brought up in a society where they are encouraged into debt. The only way to use a credit card is to **pay it off in full every month**. Now I have a confession to make, as a businessman I have a number of credit cards for the business but only one for personal use and all of them are paid off in full every month. I have a card for business fuel; so that when that bill comes in I know exactly how much I have been charged for fuel this month and can match it to my spending record. I have another card for stationery purchases and again I can match the bill with my spending record. For my personal expenses I have one card which is an annual no-fee card which, as I have said, is paid off in full every month, and I have a back up which is not used. Why do I have a backup? Just occasionally my main card is refused, it may be a bad terminal link or something else just as silly, so I always have a backup but rarely use it. In fact I am on my third back up card at the moment because the credit card companies get so fed up with me not spending that they withdraw the card. I just get another back-up card.

I came across a great idea from another author regarding credit cards. You do need one for emergencies because in reality emergencies do happen and surprisingly some places will not accept cash. This is because there are fake notes and coins in circulation and they do not wish to be caught. So what is the great idea, well it is simple, get a tin and fill it with water, put your credit card in it and then put it in your freezer. This little blighter will then freeze into a block of ice and if there is a problem that you need the card for, you will be forced to wait 24 hours until the card defrosts. That way if it is an impulse buy, the impulse will no doubt have gone and you can put the card back in the freezer, what a great idea, I am almost tempted to say 'cool'!

So what are the warning signs of being credit dependent?

You are credit dependent if:

1   you often pay for things with credit because you don't have enough money (you are spending future wages);

2   you carry the credit card balance from month to month and it is going up;

3   you are applying for new credit cards;

4   you pay for one credit card bill with another credit card;

5   you panic at the thought of never having a credit card

6   you pay your bills late. For example:
    a) you write out the cheques to pay your bills but don't post them because there is not enough in your current account;
    b) you count on next month's money to pay this month's bills;
    c) you pay half of your bills this week and half next week
    d) you regularly pay 30 days late;
    e) even if the money is in your account, you do not pay for fear something else might turn up.

7   you save nothing. OK you intend to but never quite get around to it. That is exactly the position I was in when I first met Judith. Some years earlier in a previous relationship I had developed the habit of spending more than I earned and was still doing so. If you are like me, you justify this by saying that you will save when your income exceeds your outgoings but it never happens. Remember, I am not pointing fingers here, I have been where you are and I can tell you life is a lot more pleasant

out of that situation. The other reason I heard from someone in the village where I used to live was 'The house is gaining value every year, so that is savings isn't it?'. This is the same woman I have mentioned elsewhere who spent the mortgage equity on liabilities, she increased doubled her mortgage saying 'Well it is free money', no it is not, this is silly, silly, silly;

8   you think of your credit rating as savings because it is available in case of an emergency;

9   you worry about money. Worry is a killer, when you are worried about money you are an easy target for debt because it looks like a lifesaver. There are warning signs to be aware of:
a) you are thinking of money constantly;
b) you have trouble sleeping;
c) you panic when the phone rings;
d) you hide purchases or bills from your partner;

10 you overspend on your current account. This is called being close to the edge and it is not a happy place to be. If you are getting unauthorised overdrafts on your current account or even authorised ones, you are heading into the debt trap. I once worked for an online college where I was head of mathematics. The owner seemed a nice enough guy but was a rogue and within a year the business collapsed owing me £10,000. I was so committed to the work I was absolutely flabbergasted when I presented a payment cheque (I was a freelancer) and the cheque bounced. This guy was signing cheques that he had absolutely no intention to honour. The last I heard was that he was having to sell his home to pay off debtors and I never did get my £10,000.

Have you ever dreamt of winning the lottery or getting rich quickly without worrying about money? Or you could live an extravagant lifestyle and have it all? Older readers will remember Viv Nicholson, a 1960s pools winner, who famously said she was going to 'spend, spend, spend' and boy did she spend. She had won the equivalent of what today would have been millions but in a few short years was left bankrupt. Now I have never met Ms Nicholson but I suspect the reason she spent her way back to her original financial state was to do with her attitude to money. When you have an attitude that denies the need to manage money and let it manage you, you are a fertile ground for credit. This is because easy credit tempts you to have the lifestyle now and then, when your 'ship comes in' you will pay it all off, this is really a silly idea. If you do win the lottery or the pools, then listen to the experts they supply you with, that is why they are there. They will advise you on ways to invest and maintain your new status and not waste the money. We know of one woman who won the lottery and decided to buy her council house (she was a cleaner at a school I used to teach) and she then had a £100,000 extension built on her home. This was a wonderful idea, she kept her network of friends, she helped people out financially and she enjoyed life but she controlled the money, not the other way around. In early 2009 we heard of a woman who had won £1 million and still turned up in her cafe at 5 am to cook breakfast for truckers. Again this woman has kept a sense of priority and well done to her.

Can you see these warning signs in your life? If the answer is 'yes' then well done for seeing the truth but don't panic. These warning signs are telling you it is time to take action to improve your life. If you have bypassed the warning signs and the debt prison cell has slammed behind you then again don't panic. Now is the time to start using tools to cut your way out of there and to get back to financial freedom. It can be done, I know from personal experience.

The best way forward

The better way forward is to take control of your debts. Here is a plan of action that we are going to enact together.

1   Get serious about dealing with this matter. Dealing with debt and running your household accounts is going to be a little like running a business but the business is you

limited or you PLC. In truth Judith and I refer to our personal finances as Lawler PLC and that is how you should view your own. The ultimate objective has to be that the money coming in exceeds the money going out and the excess is saved and then invested. First of all, make a personal decision and write it down in your journal, make it clear that you are going to do whatever it legally takes to clear all debts. Go on, do it now, (yes I know I am an old nagbag but hey!) and make sure you date it. This is going to be a source of inspiration and strength in the journey to financial freedom.

2   Pay yourself first. I will explain this in later chapters but you are going to need a contingency fund and a survival fund. These both have different roles to play. Remember you come first. I know this sounds a little crazy. When I first started on this road with Judith I was certain that this was wrong, we needed every penny to ensure we paid off our creditors but the reality is life is put on hold (and that my friends is no fun at all, and I mean having no fun at all).

3   Use the tracking tools to see where the money is going, I will explain these later and they are simple yet devastatingly powerful tools that anyone can use and benefit from; it is essential that you find the leaks. These are the places where money is leaking from your life and you may not even be aware of it. These are the must have purchases that you really do not need. I have already mentioned my own 'need' for computer magazines that were costing £1,500 a year but we couldn't afford a £1,500 holiday. Some people, in fact quite a lot of people believe that if they only had 25% more income everything would be OK. Let me tell you dear reader it would not be. I have met people who have said that they will feel happier when they earn more, but they never do. Happiness and security come from within not from an outside source. Happiness and security are a result of a positive self-image and realistic but positive self esteem. This means we recognise what and who we are and feel good about ourselves.

> **SUZI QUATRO**
> The rock star Suzi Quatro said 'I feel good inside my skin'.
> Ms Quatro has a wonderful sense of self-image and clearly
> has very positive mental health, which is what we all need.

4   Designing a cunning plan. Do you remember the character
    Baldrick in the *Blackadder* series, it was a running joke that
    he always had a cunning plan. For instance in the First
    World War series, Baldrick had a bullet with his name
    written on it. When asked why, he replied, 'Well you know
    they say there is a German out there somewhere with a
    bullet that has your name on it, well if I've got it he can't
    have it can he!' he would always look triumphantly at
    Blackadder who would groan at the stupidity of his
    remarks. But that is exactly what we do need here, well
    perhaps not a cunning plan but certainly a plan. You would
    never dream of building a house without a detailed plan
    and in the same way you will not build your financial
    freedom without a plan. This is a road that will take you
    where you wish to go and give you markers on the
    journey.

5   What do you actually own? You are building a road that will
    take you from debt to debt-free living so it is vital that you
    know what you own. By this I do not just mean the
    contents of your home but also your financial assets. If you
    do not know where your policies are, find them now. Who
    is the main breadwinner in your home? If it is you do you
    have dependents? If so it is essential that you have life
    assurance. I do not wish to be morbid but if anything
    untoward does happen to you, then you need to ensure
    that your dependents are protected. Remember protection
    comes before investment. Make sure that you are also
    covered at work. The real danger is not that you will be
    killed but in fact that you will be injured and being
    uninsured if you cannot continue working you are in a real
    pickle. Sticking with financial documents, do you have any
    savings from when you were a kid? What about premium
    bonds? You also need to ensure you have things like your
    birth certificate and any other so-called heritage documents
    like degree certificates and transcripts of courses.

6 Make an inventory of things you have in your home. Excluding family heirlooms and anything of sentimental value, I suggest that you have a declutter. Have a car boot sale or try Ebay for getting rid of stuff that you have not used in the last year. Remember if you have not used in the last year then it is extremely unlikely that you will ever use it again. So why not pass it on to someone else and liquidate some cash. This is a good move in that it turns clutter into cash and can help towards debt repayment. Don't forget old books, if you have read them then pass them on. A good way of raising a small amount of cash is to sell them on Amazon's marketplace. Just a word of warning though if you have a home stuffed full of novels then they are probably worthless and you might as well give them to charity. The professional sellers who sell on Amazon actually often have a contract with the Royal Mail and get their post slightly cheaper than the rest of us and so it make sense for them to sell used novels. For the rest of us the figures simply do not work. A lot of novels sell at 1p on Amazon but Amazon charge £2.75 for the book. However it is not that easy because Amazon also charge about 30p for listing the book when sold and then another take of about 30p, so that is about £1 gone. OK the postage will be about £1.20 and the bag to send it in will be about 50p so eureka you will have made about 30p, hmm hardly worth the effort. However, if you have old college or university books these are often collectibles and so can be worth far more. I once came across a German–English technical dictionary. I paid 30p for this second hand and sold it on Amazon for £63, so it can be worthwhile. Amazon is better than Ebay for books because you do not pay unless it is sold whereas with Ebay you have to pay a listing fee. I also sold a lot of old college books when I was a young teacher to a colleague and was able to pay my mortgage that month. When I say I have been where you are now I was not lying.

7 Remember *do not* incur debt today. You must not add to your debt today. Debt is like quicksand, it drags you down and if you are trying to get out of the debt swamp you will fail miserably if the plan is being sabotaged by you continuing to increase debt on a daily basis. It is like

eating. You can eat all day non-stop but you cannot be slim at the same time. You can spend all day as well but you cannot be solvent (debt free).

We heard of one story where a family was in debt but were still spending hundreds of pounds per year taking the kids to burger bars every Friday. First of all the burgers are not good for the kids, recent projections say that soon 90% of children will be obese and that means more than 30% of their body weight is fat, that is nine out of ten children and teenagers. Believe me, as a man who has struggled with weight all my life, not taking them to the burger bar is a kindness, take them to the park instead to play a ball game. It will be more fun for the whole family, it is so-called quality time and it is free.

8   Look at revenue-raising opportunities. Believe me they are out there surrounding you. I will discuss these in more detail later but it needs you to look out for them. Is there a dog walking service in your area? Could you start one? Could you do a professional job as a hairdresser? Could you decorate rooms part time? Remember, if you do any of these things you must write and let HMRC know about them. You are liable to pay tax on the earnings.

9   Persevere: in your own personal space in your home put a date on the wall, call it 'DF day', or 'Debt-free day'. This is some point in the future when you will own everything you want and owe nothing. It may take a few years and you will need to revisit your plan but it will work.

10   This is probably the most important principle, **know what you owe**. You are going to need to have a list of people/organisations to whom you owe money and you will need to write to them explaining that you are on the British back to the black programme and what this means. Don't worry, I will talk you through how to do this in later chapters.

6   **The Tools of the Trade**

Redesigning your life: Step One

Where does your money go?

Now you need to start taking control and start redesigning your life and that means controlling money not letting it control you. The first step is to determine where the money actually goes. Don't skip this, it really is a vital step to redesigning your life. I found to my own cost (literally) that when I skipped this I went back to my old ways of spending. Habits are hard to break and it does require discipline and discipline only comes with awareness. This is the first stage in raising your awareness, actually determining where the money goes. To do this you need to start a diary. Sounds crazy I know but there really is a purpose in this method. It is essential to record everything you spend. This is a simple strategy that anyone can use and you will.

Hand on heart, who taught you how to use money?

If you are like me (and I am over 40 years old), the chances are nobody. It was assumed that you would somehow acquire the skills to manage money, principally by looking at how other people did it. This is exactly what I did but when other people are doing it wrong and you copy their approach, then you end up doing it wrong too. At school we were introduced to Hardy and Shakespeare, quadratic equations and supply and demand curves but nobody ever taught us how to manage money. These days things are changing in schools and not before time, but in those days it was different. So now you need a tool, in fact you need a number of tools and the first is the daily spending record.

The daily spending record

This is a vital tool in your new approach to money. It is a simple yet devastatingly powerful tool that anyone can use and profit from when managing their money. It is essential that you are clear about where your money is going, before you can even begin to make effective changes. Other than the rent or mortgage and a vague idea about the gas or electricity bill, most people cannot tell you either how much they spend each month or on what they spend it. To give you an example of this, I went to the local gym and had to pay my annual membership. Now this is a council-run gym, not a private one obviously because these cost a huge amount more. I said to the woman at the counter as I handed over my money in the form of a £10 note that I had hoped that 'tenner would last the week'. She was amazed, she said 'I had £45 in my purse yesterday and now the whole lot is gone and I do not know where'. If ever there was a candidate for this programme, it is that lady.

So you see, the spending record is essential. Remember the marketeers, advertisers, and banks are like a young man on a 'promise' from his lovely young lady. They get wealthier as you get poorer. Think about the 'system' they use; they want you to buy all their products, they want you to clutter your home with things because the more you spend, the wealthier they become. Not only do they want you to buy it, but they will even lend you the money to buy it. We are back to credit again, what a surprise. How cool is that! Actually it is not cool at all, it is like heroin. Now I have never taken heroin but I understand it makes you feel good but each time in order to get that 'high' you have to take a little more and a little more and so it goes on, it is the same with credit. Credit is consumer smack, it gets you hooked and getting off is like going cold turkey.

So this is why you need a daily record. This is a record of the cash you spent today. Do not be confused into thinking it is a plan, it is simply a list of what you spent money on today. Just make a list of what you spend as you spend it. It may be that you decide to keep it in a spiral bound notebook, others decide to use a strip of paper kept in a pocket. On the list write today's date and then every time you buy something write down what you spent the money on, to the penny. For example:

Monday 1 March	
Newspaper	.50
Coffee	£2.75
Cigarettes	£4.80
Lunch	£5.75
Groceries	£19.79

Remember it is essential that you keep this record to the penny, otherwise you can have rounding errors and it will distort your expenditure.

Look at how easy this is, it is so powerful it is awesome and never again will you wonder where the cash went, unlike the lady at the gym. Managing your money like this is so easy, yet in management terms it is a 'new dawn' of management and it empowers you. You are in control, you are controlling the spending and not the other way around.

So keep the record, make it a daily plan and stick to it. The mark of a superior mind is to be able to focus and deliver and this is what you need to do. It means that when you buy something you record it on your daily record. Don't worry about what others think. Step aside from the queue or wait until you are in the street but it is vital that you record the expense virtually at the time of spending. Do not wait until you get home because something else will be more pressing. I actually use an envelope system in my diary where the receipt (and always ask for a receipt) goes into the envelope and I write the date and the expense on the front of the envelope. If you pay for something by cheque then there is little sense in writing in your daily record because you have it on the counterfoil in your cheque book. Make sure when writing a cheque that you always write the counterfoil first and then write out the rest of the cheque, (so what if there are other people in the queue behind you, you are an important customer too). You should also ensure that your cheque guarantee card is *not* kept with your cheque book. If you do keep them together you really are asking to be ripped off. Lose one and you lose both and some unscrupulous person will spend your money like it is going out of fashion.

Don't think you will remember what it cost later on because the chances are you will not. If you do buy on a credit card then mark that on your daily record with the abbreviation 'cc' against it. This will then be a reminder to you that not all of the money in your current account belongs to you so some of it needs to be transferred to your peace of mind (POM account, more of which later).

The weekly account

The weekly account is a summary of your daily record of expenses over a week. It is an accurate record of what you spent and where you spent it for the whole week. The best way to do this is to split the month up into four weeks recognising that the last week will not be seven days. So let's say it is August, you start your weekly record as:

August 1–7, the second week will be 8 to 14, the third week 15 to 21 and then the final week will be 22 to 31.

Write the week dates at the top of your record and then make a vertical list of the categories on which you spent money, eg mortgage/rent, utilities (gas, electricity, water), clothes, entertainment, telephone, transport, snacking (coffees, chocolate bars, etc when on the move – go on, write them down). When you have finished the record might look like this:

August 1–7	
Mortgage	£450.08
Utilities	£50.35
Clothes	£50.00
Food	£43.90
Snacking	£12.75
Transport	£25.00
Entertainment	£50.00
Telephone	£12.00

That is your weekly record. It is worth designating a place, say a drawer, in your home where the daily records are kept and then at the end of the week they need to be put onto the weekly record, but this is not the end of it.

The monthly record

This is the last one, it is a record that summarises your weekly expenses for the month. This tells you exactly how much money you have spent and where it has gone.

The monthly record for August might look like the example shown opposite.

Notice what you need to do at the end. You need to total vertical total column and the horizontal total column and the two should match. This is your check that you have correctly added the sums together. If the vertical total and the horizontal total do not match, there is an error and you need to find it.

Now you have a new tool that analyses how you actually live. It provides an insight into what you really do with your money and will probably tell you a great deal about your life, some of which you may not be aware.

	Week 1	Week 2	Week 3	Week 4	Total
Mortgage	£450.08				£450.08
Utilities	£50.35				£50.35
Clothes	£50.00				£50.00
Food	£43.90	£45.89	£40.20	£52.10	£182.09
Entertainment	£50.00	£50.00	£50.00	£50.00	£200.00
Telephone	£12.00				£12.00
Transport	£25.00	£25.00	£25.00	£25.00	£100.00
Snacking	£12.75	£10.00	£12.75	£12.50	£48.00
Totals	£694.08	£130.89	£127.95	£139.60	£1,092,52

The key to success with this system is to be precise with the categories. Did you notice how I had a category for food but a separate category for snacking? So if you went to a burger bar and bought a takeaway, then this is listed as snacking. If we included the snacking in the food category it would give a false picture. The other point it makes is that the person, let's assume it is you, for whom this is a spending record has lost sight of some basic facts of life. £12.75 is a lot of chocolate or burgers or chips or whatever, and you are wasting money. You may have even lost some of your ability to enjoy food. Did you know that in Europe instead of fast food there is a new movement called slow food? This is a movement where you are encouraged to enjoy food, to eat well and to eat cheaply.

Eating wholesome food is a pleasure, it is good for you. It is for most people an extremely enjoyable social experience. So why are you denying yourself this pleasure and eating junk? The answer is probably time (it was for me), but it is worth the effort to re-educate your taste buds, and cook at home instead of paying out £48 per month on snacking. This £48 would buy another week's worth of groceries, so why not eat in and enjoy Thai Chicken with a lemon-based sauce on a bed of Pillau rice, it is delightful! This meal works out cheaper than two burgers and is both more enjoyable and better for you. I must confess to being anti-burger anyway. I have only ever had one burger from a well-known burger bar (I wanted to see what the fuss was all about). When I bit into it, the fat ran down both sides of my face, it was vile and a waste of money. The point is, the desperation of debt can often result in a deterioration of life and that includes the quality of food that we eat. This often increases stress, decreases energy and brings a gloom down on daily life. It is something to be aware of and to plan to avoid.

Notice there is an entertainment category. This is essential; you must *not* put life on hold. It is vital that you have a sense of fun in life and you must play. In the example I put £50 per week, this is excessive for me. I live in a quiet part of Wales and we certainly do not spend that sort of money on entertainment. However, in a big city like London, Cardiff, Glasgow or Belfast this is certainly possible. One word of warning though, you must keep this to a maximum of 10% of your weekly net income (after tax). This is vital if you want to become debt free. Otherwise you are just kidding yourself.

So using a calculator, take the take-home pay for a week and divide it by ten. This is 10% of your take home pay and this is the **maximum** you can afford to spend on entertainment.

> If you are self employed then you need to deduct 30% of any income immediately and place it in a high interest account. This is to cover your tax and National Insurance liabilities. Do not be tempted to touch this money, it is not yours, it belongs to HMRC and the taxmen will soon put out their hand for it. Only then do you calculate 10% of what is left. You must cover your tax obligations first.

The more precise you are with your categories, the more accurate your spending picture will become and it is a tool to create the debt-free life you desire.

As I write, we have worked through this programme and paid off our debts. I have no personal debt at all other than the mortgage on the house, which we are now tackling. My wife Judith and I have also exchanged several thousands of pounds worth of debt into net worth. We have assets that bring in income, all of this was achieved in four years. You could do the same.

If you do not start and keep a spending record, you will never be certain where the money goes and you will always be in debt.

Dealing with hazardous plastic

Now remember, credit is like heroin, it is addictive, it is consumer smack, so do you really need a credit card? I have said earlier that you need two cards, *but* this is a question that only you can answer, do you trust yourself yet? The point is can you go out with two cards in your wallet or purse and *not* use them. Be honest, because it is only yourself you are fooling. If the answer is no then you need the tin trick. In case you are skipping through the book then the tin trick was mentioned elsewhere but briefly it involves getting an old washed-out tin, filling it with water and putting your cards in it. Then put it in the freezer. The cards will freeze in a block of ice and stop you using them on an impulse. I now trust myself to use the card correctly so as I have mentioned I have a personal card and a back-up card. The personal card is used for the times when Judith sends me out to buy things we forget to get or when I need to buy clothes and things like that, but I *do not* impulse buy any more. As I have said before I once belonged to five bookclubs and no one needs five bookclubs, so don't go there my friend. If you feel confident that you can avoid impulse buys then go ahead and carry the card and use it for the purpose for which it was designed, but **it must be paid off at the end of the month in full**.

If you are at a point where you have some control but not total control then:

1   keep it in a drawer and take it out **only** when it is needed;

2   know exactly what you intend to use it for, before it goes into your purse or wallet and make sure it goes back into the drawer when you return;

3   do not use it for anything else other than the intended purpose;

4   make a deduction from your current account to cover this expense as soon as you get back home.

Believe in yourself, you do have talent.
Dr Graham Lawler
aka Mr Educator

This last point is essential if you are to avoid falling into the daily debt trap, remember we have been there and it is no fun.

Prepaid cash cards

As we were preparing this book we heard of prepaid cash cards and hidden charges. These are cards like credit cards that are 'loaded' with cash. They have been common in colleges for about the last ten years or so where students use them to buy food in the canteen and snacks from the shop, etc. What is not as well know is often these cards carry hidden charges. Some of them charge £2.50 every time you use the card. So you spend £1 and you are charged £2.50, so the £1 item is suddenly £3.50. You really do need to **read the small print**.

The banking crisis that started in 2007

You would have to be living on Mars not to know how the financial world collapsed around us at the end of 2007. Well some of us (me) did say in 2005 that we are heading for economic melt-down and I was laughed at and called delusional. As I said above, I did not spot the sub-prime scandal, but it was obvious that there was a 'bubble' in place. (A 'bubble' is an economic term for the over valuation of something, in this case it was property.) This means that the market has to right itself and the only way to do that is for these items to fall in value to what their true value should be. This is why property in the UK, along with many other countries, has fallen in value by substantial amounts.

The effect of this is that one morning we woke up and heard the BBC business editor Robert Peston tell us we were now officially broke. So in late 2008 and early 2009 there were major government initiatives in both the UK and the USA. You can argue about the political nature of these decisions but the one effect on debt reduction has been that we now have historically unheard of interest rate levels. For the first time in the history of the Bank of England interest rates dropped below 2%.

This has had a major effect on debt reduction and the approach people like me advise you to take, so I am going to try to give you two ways forward. You are will need to choose which way is best for you.

Two types of fund

Traditionally, the advice you are normally given for debt reduction is that you need three accounts. The first is your **current account**; you also need a **contingency fund** and a

peace of mind (POM) account. You need to ensure that you live on a maximum of 80% of your take-home pay. This is a hard and fast rule that must never be broken. In reality, many people are living on 122% of their pay, which is why they are using credit and that is unsustainable and has to stop. As a nation, we have fallen from having 6% savings to zero (according to some sources), so we need to get back up to 6% and beyond. As I have already said, if you are self-employed then you need to deduct 30% first of all. This belongs to HMRC; it does not belong to you. Then work out 80% of what is left.

This leaves 20% for you, well perhaps not quite. There are poor souls in the world with a lot less than you and you, like the rest of us, have a responsibility to pay something, so I am suggesting that at least 1% should be gifted to charity. No I am not crazy, this is 1p in every pound and of course you can do it. This leaves 19% of your income to save and pay off debt. This is where uncertain times change the approach for some people. Savings rates are very low, yet loan rates are relatively high. For example, a major high street bank is advertising a loan rate of 7.9%.

So we have a dilemma, we have debt to pay off and savings to make but if we are saving at these low rates and paying what is frankly a relatively high loan rate (guess who is paying for the banks' mess up in the financial crisis – you and me when we use credit). Should we use all of our 19% to pay off debt? If you use all of the 19% you pay off the debt far more quickly but, in the event of a crisis, you will not have a contingency or POM fund.

This is the choice you have to make.

Setting up a contingency fund

A contingency fund is at least three months' pay that you have saved. This is your survival fund. In the event of a crisis it means you have something to draw on. If you are an employee your contingency fund must be at least three months' salary, if you are self employed it should be at least six months' income. This is a 'do not touch' fund unless everything goes pear shaped and by this I mean you lose your job or your business is in trouble.

In January 2009 the BBC carried a report on the six o'clock news of a Northeast business who sold baby care products. The woman who owned the business said she had not had a customer in two weeks. She had zero takings. In this scenario the contingency fund kicks in. It means that she should have six months' money ready to draw on, to survive the slow down. I say six months here because she is self-employed.

On the same news bulletin there were a number of people who had been forced to accept four-day working week, simply because there was no demand for the products they were making. One man said his earnings were down £250 per month Again, this is where the contingency fund kicks in, it gives you a breathing space while getting over the problem or looking for more work. This is why this fund is so important, it is protection and you owe it to yourself and your family to ensure that you are protected.

The peace of mind (POM) account

A POM account is where you make a regular payment to the account to cover the irregular bills like the annual car service or MOT, the annual council tax bill, the quarterly electricity bill. It is not a savings account. It is what businesses call a 'contra account'. This means it is money that whilst it has not yet left you is allocated to a specific bill that is due soon. So you need to open up a separate account in your name and this is your POM account. Your POM account needs to be a monthly payment that will cover these costs. You need to ensure that this is not tied up in an investment-type savings account because you need ready access to it in order to pay bills. While it may be possible to pay it into an account that pays interest, do ensure there is no time delay for withdrawals.

To work out your monthly payment POM account you need to annualise the total of these bills and divide by 12. This means you need to determine what these bills are. For example, bills for:

- electricity/gas;
- council tax;
- car maintenance;
- car tax;
- personal insurance;
- water rates;
- gym membership;
- club membership.

In other words, all the bills that come in at odd times of the year and that you only pay once. Total these and then add 10%, so they might look like this:

Electricity £25 per quarter, annualised	£100
Gas £40 per quarter, annualised	£160
Council tax	£560
Car maintenance	£300
Car tax	£185
Personal insurance	£125
Water rates	£55
Gym membership	£120
Golf club social membership	£25

Each of these categories is a cost centre. The way to think of this is they are sub-accounts of the main account.

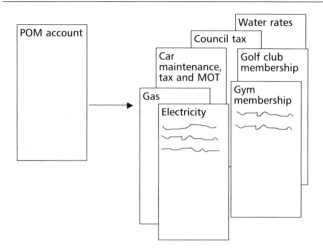

Total these and then add 10% and then divide by 12. The total is £1,070, then add 10% to this (multiply by 1.1).

These figures may be estimates at the start but you will need to refine them to make them as accurate as possible. The way to do this is to look back through past bills and total the bills per category for that year, then multiply by the inflation rate. Say you add up your electricity bills for the last year and they come to £75 in total, and on the day we did this inflation was 2%, then multiply the 75 by 1.02 (this is working out 102% of 75) and the answer is £76.50. This year, if you use the same amount of electricity, you should expect bills of £76.50 and that should be reflected in your POM account. (I wish my electricity bill was only £76.50 per year!)

The total is now £1,177. Divide this by 12 = £98.08 to the nearest penny. This means you should be paying your POM account £98.08 every month and when a bill comes in, there are funds there to pay it. Remember this is *not* a savings account; it is an account from which you will pay bills. The 10% is both a contingency (not to be confused with the contingency fund see below) to cover something that you may have missed and is also a hedge against inflation. Inflation is low at the moment but I am old enough to remember inflation rates of 25%+ so that is why I build this into my system.

The new world post-2007

In 2007 the banking crisis happened and the financial world changed. By 2009 we had the previously unheard-of low interest rates whilst loan rates remained high. This means that relative to savings, credit is incredibly expensive. So you have to make a choice. The choice is simple. In a rapid repayment plan (RRP) if you pay off the debt and create a contingency and a POM fund at the same time, then it will take longer to clear the debt, quite simply because some of the money is going into the savings accounts (contingency and POM) and not everything is going to pay off the debt. Some people argue that it makes more sense to use all of the available 19% of your income to pay off the debt in total. The effect of this is to pay off all of the debt at a faster rate *but* you will not have a contingency fund and you will not have a POM fund until you have paid off the debts. You can then use the money you were using to pay off the debt to create the POM and contingency funds.

The danger of the second method is that you have a need for a contingency whilst you are paying off the debt. The effect of this is that you have no choice – you *must* use the frozen credit card. Effectively you are getting into debt again, but remember you have no choice. If there is an emergency then you need to deal with it. So while mathematically this does make sense, there are other issues to bear in mind and one of them is learning the new psychology of not getting into debt on a daily basis. This, in our case, was made easier as we could see savings grow. It meant that we could envision a future where we would be debt free and then move on to have investments. The feeling of climbing out of debt is important. I suggest that if you pay off all the debt with the 18% of income we have identified then in fact you will still be living the debtors' lifestyle, since there is no way you can move to a largely cash-based lifestyle. However, you must decide and it does depend on the size of your debts. Either way, whether you delay creating a contingency and POM account for the moment whilst you pay off the debt, you will need to reinstate them as soon as the final debt is paid off, so for the rest of this explanation I am going to concentrate on the B2b method where we develop a contingency and POM fund alongside paying off debt.

Living on the edge

Living on the edge is said by people who do it, to be the most exciting place to be. Don't believe it, it is not. I have been there and I never want to go there again. When I was a young teacher living in Loughborough my mate Barry Thomas and I would go out drinking on a Saturday night. In reality this meant counting the coppers to see if we could afford two half pints of beer between us, sometimes we couldn't. Living on the edge means struggling from month to month and hoping and in my case even praying that I could get through. When you go over the edge then there is little choice but to jump into the dark abyss and hope to find something to cling onto on the way down, or run for the credit cards or the bank overdraft.

In my case it was both and then it took about two years to pay this off. This is how my life went on for years. It was not really through profligate spending, it was more the case that I was bachelor living alone and having to set up my own home on a non-existent budget. I soon realised that people setting up home together and getting married get far more help than single guys or girls (families and friends buy the wedding list, why isn't there a single person setting up home list?) and at that time I had just come out of a bad relationship and really wasn't in any fit state to start another one. Thankfully I have a great supportive family and they helped out a lot. Mum and Dad gave me a lot of furniture which I carried from Wales to Loughborough and we still have a lot of it, over 20 years later now that we are back in Wales. I also had good friends in Loughborough, particularly Jeff and Margaret Bestwick and their daughter Kate and her husband Graeme who were very kind to me and were a great source of support when I needed it. Believe me, anyone who sets up home on their own needs a great family of their own and a great set of friends like my friends the Bestwicks.

If you are near the edge then you need to move away from it, sooner rather than later. By creating space between you and the edge you create a stress-free buffer zone and it means you sleep well at night. So this is why you need a contingency fund and a POM account. I know I have mentioned these above but I want to recap some of the points mentioned above and go into greater detail.

The contingency fund

The contingency fund is what moves you from the edge. It is protection money, in the same way as people in the movies (and often in real life) pay thugs protection, this is your protection money. It is a second account, different from your current account that pays interest that is at least equal to inflation. But it must not be tied up, you need to get access to it when you need it. This is imperative, the contingency fund is emergency money and everyone gets emergencies at some time or other in their lives. This is not investment money or retirement savings and it is not the money that is set aside for irregular expenses. It is also *not* for discretionary spending, it is **emergency money**. I know I keep banging on about this but it is vital that this is seared across your mind. This is catastrophe money, money that you use to avoid sprinting for the frozen credit card. Remember this needs to be at least three months' salary (six months' for self-employed people) and by that I mean net or take-home pay. This is the money that keeps you if something catastrophic happens such as being 'downsized' (a euphemism for losing your job). Your contingency fund is personal debt insurance; it means you never need to get into debt when there is an emergency.

Building your contingency fund

This causes consternation with some people but you pay you first. Your income is 100% of your income. Let's say after tax you earn £1,200 – this is 100% of your net pay. You *must* live on a maximum of 80%. This leaves 20%. The function of this 20% is to do four things. First of all, 1% is for charity, that leaves 19% for three functions: building a contingency fund, building a POM account and debt repayment.

'Are you crazy Graham? I can't do that.' Yes, you can, first of all work out 80% of your income. Using the example above:

80% is 0.8 so $0.8 \times £1,200 = £960$

Therefore, there is a maximum of £960 to live on for the month, which leaves £240.

This is the money we are going to play with. Now 1% is £2.40 so go on for goodness sake give £2.40 to guide dogs for the blind or something like life boats or whatever, you can afford it and it will make you feel better. Don't worry, there will be plenty for your needs, this way you are making a small amount available for those less fortunate.

Creating the contingency fund

Three months' salary for most people will be about (I am guessing) £4,000–£5,000 and if you have no savings it may be that you are still shaking your head and telling me this cannot happen. Yes it can, have a little faith. OK remember our 18:19:1 formula, you live on a maximum of 80% of your income after tax. You then give away 1% and you are then left with 19%. From the example above, this leaves £237.60 to create a contingency fund, a POM fund and debt repayment. Remember contingency is protection so this should come first; this should be 10% of your take-home pay.

In our example this was £1200, so 10% of £1,200 is £120. Every month you will put £120 into your contingency fund and **leave it there**. The purpose is to make a pot of loot that is equal to at least three months' take-home pay. In this example that is $3 \times £1,200$ or £3,600.

So, how many months will that take?

Month	Contingency (£)
1	120
2	240
3	360
4	480
5	600
6	720
7	840
9	960
10	1,080
11	1,200
12	1,320
13	1,440
14	1,560
15	1,680
16	1,800
17	1,920
18	2,040
20	2,160
21	2,280
22	2,400
23	2,520
24	2,640

25	2,760
26	2,880
27	3,000
28	3,120
29	3,240
30	3,360
31	3,480
32	3,600

Bingo, stop the clock, you have made it. In less than three years in this example we have gone from nothing and created a pot of loot that will protect us if a catastrophe occurs. Remember to make sure your contingency is equivalent to your three months' of pay and not simply use the example here. It means that by saving a small amount of your salary (and you can do it, honestly you can), you have created a safety net. You may be tempted to see your contingency plan as a long-term investment, it is *not*. It is emergency money and only emergency money. You need to ensure that the fund is safely parked and I highly recommend that you avoid speculating with it. Use it for what it is, a safety net.

Do not be tempted to place it in a high-interest overseas account. Overseas accounts may look tempting but they are not always guaranteed by the government and if the banks go down as happened in Iceland (the country not the food store) in 2008, you risk losing all of your money. If you keep your contingency in a UK high street bank, the government guarantees it, so in the event of the bank going down you lose nothing. Make sure you keep this fund liquid; this means you need to get your hands on it within 24 hours maximum. Hopefully you will never use your contingency fund but you will need to maintain it for many years.

Ideally you want it to be exposed to the best compound interest available for no fees. I am a big fan of standing orders and I would suggest you make sure there is a standing order every month from your current account to wherever you keep your contingency fund. That way you will treat it as a regular bill and know that it is being paid. You can even authorise the number of payments, in our example above that would be 32 payments.

In the event of an emergency this pot of loot is designed to support you but when the emergency is over you need to put the money back. So after an emergency you have a responsibility to save that portion of income and again put it away for future emergencies and, make no mistake, they will occur. You also need to ensure that if, once your contingency fund is secure, your monthly pay increases that this increase is reflected in the size of your contingency fund. So, if your take home pay goes up from £1,200 a month to £1,500 a month then your contingency fund should swell from £3,600 to £4,500, to reflect this new level of income. This is a vital part of your overall money management strategy. There will come a time when you have paid up your contingency fund *but* you still need to pay yourself that 10% it cannot be used for living expenses. Remember: this is what is creating the space between you and the edge.

The POM account

This is your peace of mind fund. This should be funded from the 80% of the income on which you live. Remember this is for regular but not monthly bills, such as electricity/ gas bills, water rates, council tax or whatever. It is not 'treat' money; it is money that has a specific focus. We talked about this earlier in the book but you may need to look back at this now (pages 83–84).

Now you need to talk about debt. We still have 9% to play with, this is £108, in our example.

Listing the debt

You now need to make a list of your creditors and I mean *all* of them. Don't be frightened of this, nothing you are doing here will make your situation worse, it cannot hurt you. These debts already exists, so long as you are *not* adding to them we can deal with them together, remember I am with you all the way. If you don't know what you are working with you will not be able to plan a way forward. At this stage we really do not care about repayment, this is still the analysis stage and it is vital that we do this properly.

Make your debt list on paper with the name of the creditor on the left and the amount owed on the right. The easiest way to do this is to categorise the debts, so put all the credit cards on first. Then all the other categories, say car-associated debt, and then leisure associated debt, and so on. If you have more than one debt for the same creditor make sure you list them separately. Most people have a current account with an automatic overdraft to a certain facility. This means the bank has agreed to honour cheques up to a predetermined value, say £250. This is on the expectation that next month's income will come in and cover this debt. So make sure it is listed in your debt. Your list may look something like this:

July

Halifax credit card	£400
GM credit card	£550
Barclaycard	£1,275

> Can you see the pattern? Look at how easy they make it for us to slide into debt. Why do they do it? Because, as I have said before, they are making money out of us every time we borrow money.

Store cards

List each department store where you have a store card and the outstanding balance on each account.

Student loan

If you have a student loan, list it and the outstanding balance.

Personal loans

By this we mean loans from family and friends. If you owe more than one amount to the same person then add them up and list them once but do not add amounts owed to more than one person. So maybe Dad lent you £500 and then a further £750 so the list shows Dad is owed £1,250. Just make sure you list a separate entry for each person from whom you have borrowed.

Salary advances

If you have had an advance from your employer whether in terms of wages, salary or commission, then make sure it is listed.

Rendered services

List each organisation or individual from whom you have received a service and to whom you owe money. These can include the electrician, Corgi gas fitter, TV aerial repair company, plumber, car mechanic and so on.

Rent/mortgage

If you are in arrears then write down the amount that is outstanding.

Income tax

If you are employed this is not an issue since this tax is deducted at source, but if you are self employed then write down the back taxes you owe to HMRC.

Council tax

If you are late paying the council tax then write down exactly how much tax you owe.

Utilities

List any overdue bills for gas, electricity, telephone and water rates, if you are liable for them.

Miscellaneous

This is the catch-all category that shows the idiosyncrasy of each of our lives. In this section include any 'others' not included above. Do make sure you write each creditor's name and the amount owed and then total the amount for this section.

This is the moment of truth, total everything. Go on, you can do it, just total the lot and write it down. Now sit back and take a few breaths, this is not the end of the world, in fact it is the beginning of a new life for you, all it means is you owe some money. It will not lead to ground-to-air missiles being launched, there will not be hunter-killer submarines from Faslane searching for you, so calm down just realise that **the figure is unimportant**.

No matter what the figure is, this is what you owe. The amount is larger than for some other people but smaller than for many. What matters is that you have quantified your debt and can now take action to remove it. The point to remember is that this amount represents the amount of credit-fuelled destruction you have to remove from your life. As long as you are no longer increasing your debt you can certainly have a debt-free future.

Avoid making false promises

When you are in debt it is very easy to make false promises to creditors. When you get angry letters and demands it is extremely easy to cave in and make promises that you cannot fulfil, *do not do it* unless you are 100% sure you can keep your promise. Say you owe John's Video Rental £15 and you say 'OK John, I will post you a cheque, it will be with you on Friday' *but* you know in your heart that you are not going to do this because there is no money to pay for it. What do you think John will think of you? He will immediately think you have lied. When I was freelancing for an online college I spoke to the owner who promised faithfully that the cheque would be in the post, it was not. He had no intention of paying up and I never did get my money, you do not want to damage your good name like this man did to his name.

Creating your debt list

Now that you have a handle on what you are spending, it is time to grasp exactly how much debt you have. This is nothing to be frightened of, it is the mark of a superior mind to take control, to analyse and to plan the way forward. As I have said before in this book and in *Understanding the Numbers*, I have been where you are now. I have racked up debt and not understood where or how I got to that position. Fortunately I married a great woman and together we have rebuilt our lives. Getting out of debt is an ongoing process and one that you can do.

Take all your credit card receipts and statements and get them in weekly and monthly order. Put each bundle into a separate envelope and label each envelope with the name of the credit card company.

Take the credit card for that company and cut it up and put it into the envelope. Go on, you can do it, you can cut it up and you can be debt free. Remember we have already agreed that we will no longer incur debt. There is no longer a need to get further into debt, but there is a need to pay off the debts and so make sure you cut that card up, now go on, put down this book and get the scissors and cut the little blighter in bits. Make sure you cut horizontally through the numbers and your name and then cut these vertically, that way nobody will be able (without a lot of work) to reassemble them and scam you. Now put those bits into the envelope with the statements and on the front of the envelope write the date and the amount owed. Remember credit cards are consumer smack (the slang name for heroin), they are designed to get you hooked. They will not make you rich, they will not increase your wealth, the function of that card is to **take money away from you**, so why on earth would you want to keep using them? So go on, cut them up now.

CREDIT CARDS AND DEBIT CARDS
Remember you are going to get rid of all of your credit cards except two and these need to be two without fees and they need to incur the lowest interest rate. Having said that, since you are going to pay off the full amount when the bill is due each month that is not as important as it was. These two cards are to be used *only* in times when there is no alternative. As I have said elsewhere there are times when shops will not accept cash and so a card is essential *but it must be paid off in full*. You will only use one of the cards, the other is a back-up if the first one is refused.

A better choice is to use a debit card. This is a card from your bank where the money is taken directly from your account so you can record this as a cash spend on your daily spending record. This is how we pay for our groceries at the supermarket each week. We always pay with a debit card so that we know the bill is clear. However, there is one circumstance where credit cards are better than debit cards and that is buying online. When you buy using a credit card the credit card company insures you so if the product does not arrive, then you can claim your money back from the credit card company. Do you remember in 2000 there was such a lot of talk about the millennium bug? We received an unsolicited letter from a man who said he was selling a piece of software that 'eliminated all risk' from the millennium bug. So, since we are both heavy computer users, Judith and I decided to buy. We sent off our money (we were far more innocent in those days) and surprise, surprise no software arrived. Following a number of calls to the phone number we were given we still received no response and no software and it was only by complaining to the credit card company that we got our money back. The credit card company told me they went 'into' this account and reversed the transaction. The seller operated under an alias and he was and still is well known by Port Talbot Trading Standards to whom we also complained. Following our successful claim against him he then wrote to me saying that the disc carrying the software had been dispatched but had 'obviously been lost in the post' and that consequently he was 'taking the loss'. Funny how he did not respond to my phone calls prior to the money being reclaimed but there we are, such is life!

By now you should have a set of envelopes with the credit card statement for each card in its own envelope and inside is the cut up card. You should have two envelopes with cards that are not cut up. These are the no-fee cards that you will use. Both of them need to be in your wallet but only for emergencies. Decide which one you will use and keep the other for back-up in case the first one is refused. You need a credit card to shop online, so despite what some financial experts say, this is important. But remember, **you must be able to pay it off at the end of the month**. We have talked about the 80:19:1 rule later, this must come out of the 80.

Now you need to think about debt repayment, you have made superb progress since you first started this book. Look at what you have covered. You have examined your relationship to money, you have been introduced to the techniques needed for managing money and you are already on the road to recovery. The next step is to have a debt repayment plan and that is what I have called the RRP or rapid repayment plan. Do remember that you can, once through this phase, go on to have a life full of abundance and security; this is the last step to take.

8

Stabilising

The spending plan

Notice that I refer to a spending *plan* not a budget, a *plan*. This is exactly how top companies plan their spending for a year. They often look at the year ahead and then at their costs and plan exactly what must be earned each month in order for those targets to be achieved. I once worked for a company in Cheltenham where they set a target turnover and profit level each year and then worked flat out to achieve it by keeping costs low and revenue streams high. This is exactly the same principle for your home money management system. You have most of the tools ready, you have a contingency fund in development, you have a POM fund in development and in this chapter we are going to plan spending. Have you ever got into the 'I can't afford it' mode of thinking?

I remember as a child this was a regular mantra in our house and while it was probably true, it was certainly depressing. This sense of impoverished living can actually lead to further debt. The reasoning is simple – I can afford it on the credit card. In other words, this kind of thinking can and often does lead to debt. In reality each of us can afford a lot more than we think. In *Understanding the Numbers* I talked about a guy I knew who was vocal in his comments about our going to the Canary Islands for holidays. He said 'You can only afford that because you do not have kids'. However, this man has thousands of pounds worth of music CDs. He has no problem in finding £18 for an impulse buy of a CD to add to his collection. The fact is he *chooses* to spend his money on music, we choose to have a holiday in the Canaries, in fact I am sitting in our apartment in the Canaries as I write this and enjoying the sunshine. He took his family on a UK holiday because with 'Two kids you can't go abroad, can you? It is just too expensive'. So he has stopped thinking about the reality of his situation and started to bemoan his lot. The fact is he could have a holiday abroad with his family but he chooses to have thousands of pounds worth of music instead. The same man wanted a new car, why? Well the heated front window of his car had packed in. I had a solution, a 50p tea towel.

My current car is my sixth car in a 30-year driving career and it is the first car with a heated front window. For the first five cars I carried an old tea towel and wiped the front window down. In fact it was only my third car that had a fully functioning rear window and still had to have the front window wiped by a towel.

What happened to this man was his car front window heater packed in and so he decided he had to have it fixed. The problem was that the unit, although it cost only 50p, was buried deep within the engine and so the labour charge would have been almost £2,000 to replace a 50p unit. His response was 'buy a new car'. The rest of his old car was fine *but* because it was not 'pristine' it was not good enough. This is crazy thinking. He chooses to spend thousands on a new car because a unit has gone but says he cannot afford to take his family abroad.

The fact is we have choices on how to spend our money and yes, it does include cars and yes, it does include music but it also includes holidays. If a family holiday is very important to you and your family's sense of well-being, then you should and must plan for it. Once you recognise and accept the fact that you do have choices about how you spend your money and that although you have made certain choices in the past there is no reason for you to keep making the same choices, then you will begin to make more pleasing and satisfying choices.

A simple example of this is a woman who ordered her Christmas turkey. She said 'We always have a big bird at Christmas although we get sick of eating turkey after four days.'

Her 14-year-old son said, 'So why do we have a big bird?'

'We always have a big bird.'

'But why?'

'Because we always do.'

This woman was so conditioned to making the same choices for Christmas that she simply hadn't considered choosing anything else. The idea of having a smaller bird so the family would no longer be 'sick of turkey' had not entered her head. When we probed deeper it turns out that as a child her parents had always had a big bird because her father was a butcher and as a member of staff you were often given Christmas turkeys that simply could not be sold. This had become a tradition in childhood and had continued even though the family did not really want such a huge bird. How many decisions that you make are conditioned by your childhood experiences?

In the same way, years of living with debt can condition you to behave in a similar manner. The first and easiest answer, often without having to think of it is, 'we can't afford it', when often we can. Remember there is not a lot that you are compelled to do with your money, there is a lot that you choose to do, so what is the way forward? It is to have a spending plan.

Remember the monthly record? (See page 76.)

This is our example from earlier in the book. You should use your own monthly record. Using the monthly record you are now going to develop a spending plan. This is a set of cost centres, in other words they are categories for which you are going to plan to spend money on. Each cost centre is like a sub account of the main account. You need to write down what you intend to spend or plan to spend in

	Week 1	Week 2	Week 3	Week 4	Total
Mortgage	£450.08				£450.08
Utilities	£50.35				£50.35
Clothes	£50.00				£50.00
Food	£43.90	£45.89	£40.20	£52.10	£182.09
Entertainment	£50.00	£50.00	£50.00	£50.00	£200.00
Telephone	£12.00				£12.00
Transport	£25.00	£25.00	£25.00	£25.00	£100.00
Snacking	£12.75	£10.00	£12.75	£12.50	£48.00
Totals	£694.08	£130.89	£127.95	£139.60	£1,092,52

the next month or week, whichever is best for you. Here we are going to do it for month one and we will combine the spending plan with the record of the week. Don't forget you may have a lot more categories than this. For instance, what about books, child support, house equipment, laundry, personal care and so on. Just remember the total of your spending plan cannot be more than 80% of your earnings after deductions, namely your net income.

Month

	1	2	3	4	Planned actual +/-
Mortgage/rent					
Contingency					
POM					
Utilities					
Clothes					
Food					
Entertainment					
Telephone					
Transport					
Snacking					
Giving					

Remember you have committed to not increasing your debt today, so this bit should be easy. Take last month's spending record and look at the amounts that you actually spent. Look at each category one at a time, how realistic is this? Did you notice how we added two more categories to the spending plan? The contingency fund and the POM are listed because these are cost centres that you will need to cater for and they should come second after your mortgage or rent, that is why we have added them after the mortgage/ rent line. The mortgage/rent and your contingency form are what we can consider your fixed costs. They should not vary much and you do need to keep a roof over your head, protect yourself with the contingency and have peace of mind in the future, hence the POM. Notice there is also a category for giving, in this case we are giving away 1% or 1p in every pound to charity, so this month we will aim to give £10.92. Did you also notice that in the spending plan we have a total of £1,092? This is 91% of the take-home pay you receive, the rest will be used for debt repayment and we will deal with that later.

In the example above we said we spent £12.50 on snacking. Now ask yourself if this is too much or too little or about right? Only you can decide that, for me this is far too much. If you agree with me then you would reduce it. For me £10 a week maximum is enough to contribute to chocolate or whatever, so I then multiply this by four because there are four weeks on our plan.

So now I put £40 against snacking under the planned and now my spending plan looks like this:

Month

	1	2	3	4	Planned actual +/-
Mortgage/rent					£560.00
Contingency					£120.00
POM					£98.08
Utilities					
Clothes					
Food					
Entertainment					
Telephone					

Transport	
Snacking	£40.00
Giving	£10.92
Total	£1,092.00

I now need to go through all of the other categories and make the same judgement. Do I want to spend the same as I did last month on this category, more than I did last month or less than I did last month?

Now here comes the sticky bit, when you first do this it is quite likely that you will go over the total amount planned. If this is the case, you have to go back through the categories and prune back somewhere. It is essential that you understand this, these are hard and fast rules to get you from where you are to where you want to be, namely debt free and it is essential that you stick to these rules. They really do work – they have worked for me and they can work for you as well.

You cannot take home £1,200 and spend £1,350 in a month without incurring debt. For me the places to cut would be telephone (cut down the time you use the phone or try texting) transport (take the bus or walk) and probably entertainment (eat in rather than going out to eat). But do not remove all the entertainment from your life, as my good friend the well know therapist Deborah Harty puts it, you must remember to play (see www.deborahharty.co.uk). I cannot stress this too much. When I first moved to Loughborough, I was so broke and so much in debt I did not go out for nearly two years other than the occasional ½ pint of beer in the pub and suffered a major depression that lasted for about six months. I was earning £300 a month as a young single teacher and immediately I got paid my mortgage was paid and I was still £300 in debt. It was so bad I was called into the bank to explain myself. In the bank I told the cashier that I did not live 'high on the hog'. They actually congratulated me for staying so little in debt, but it was not a consolation. So, under no circumstances whatsoever should you cut your entertainment budget totally, it is essential to your sense of well-being and must be part of your spending plan. The purpose of this programme is to improve the quality of your life and not to reduce it. Look at the really boring areas of your expenditure, can you reduce these and then spend the savings on the areas that give you pleasure?

If, however, you have been extravagant in the past in the areas of pleasure, then you will have to cut these back.

> In *Understanding the Numbers* I mentioned a young man who lived in London. He enjoyed coffee and cake but at London prices this was costing him £16 a time and he was doing it four times a day, this is £64 per day or £320 per week or £1280 a month. Not exactly sensible. It would have been far cheaper for him to learn how to bake his own cakes.

You must not put off developing a spending plan and as you do it you should ensure that the total for the month should not exceed 91% of the total of your take-home income. Even if you are 1p over, then you are incurring debt and remember you do not do this any more.

For me this stage was a reality check, I simply, or so I thought, could not manage on what I was earning. In fact I was choosing to have a car so that I could get to school to earn money to pay for the car, hmmm, makes you think doesn't it? At this stage I did the only thing I could and looked for ways to increase my income.

If your expenses are greater than your income and you have savings, then you can draw on those savings. That is allowed because it is not incurring more debt, which is why we have the contingency fund. But this is hardly a good strategy because the savings will dwindle away. It is far better to decrease expenditure on certain areas or increase income.

How can you cut expenses?

- Car share; for many years I shared trips to and from school with two other teachers.

- Use the bus service rather than take a taxi or, if you are in a city, use the underground or tram service.

- Walk instead of taking a bus.

- Go to watch a film rather than go out to a restaurant (on my 49th birthday Judith and I went to see the James Bond film *A Quantum of Solace* rather than as going out for a meal as we usually did. At that time a meal would have cost about £50 but we saw the film for about £12. This resulted a substantial saving.

- Rent a DVD rather than go to the movies.

- Entertain at home rather than go out.

- Wear last year's clothes for a little longer.

- Send emails or texts rather than calling people long distance.

- Keep a scrupulous daily spending record.

- Cancel non-essential services like lawn maintenance. (Well done to the guy from North Wales who brought that service from the USA, he is now said to be worth £130 million and he reportedly started out with a bag of lawn fertiliser in the back of a Ford Sierra.)

- Borrow books from the library rather than buying them.

- Buy used books from Amazon for 1p plus the postal charge (currently £2.75) so for £2.76 (about the price of a pint of beer) you get a novel delivered to your door and about four hours of pleasure from reading it. That really is cheap entertainment. (Look out for Lime Avenue Books on amazon.co.uk, that is Judith's business.)

- Stop smoking: seriously it is killing you, you will probably may not live to see your children grow up and have children of their own and you are paying a fortune for it. It is the one legal product that kills the people who use it.

- Use parks and council facilities like council gyms for sport and exercise rather than private facilities.

- Use museums as part of your entertainment, they are free (remember the Hamiltons when they were broke, advertising museums in London?)

- Repair damaged items like clothes rather than replace them.

All of the above will make substantial savings. One other thought: if you have children it is often easy to have the 'hand me down' syndrome, but the younger child can start to feel second best when all she or he gets are the old clothes from an older child. It is important for their sense of self-esteem that they get new things as well. Children can be thoughtless and it is quite common for older children to taunt the younger ones with comments such as 'You get all my old rubbish'. When you are a child you can feel vulnerable and totally under-valued and it is vital that you show your child they are valued. On a personal level I must also say, if you have two children of about the same age and same sex, do avoid dressing them identically. From personal experience I can tell you it is no fun for the child, it makes the child entertainment for adults with 'Oh, don't they look alike' and can affect their developing sense of identity. If you want to show each is valued then make sure they are aware that you have planned to spend exactly the same on each of them but let them be different. They are different people and are not clones of each other. It really is that vital to have your own sense of identity. Anyone who scoffs at this has not thought it through. Women will understand the feeling of being 'John's wife' rather than having an identity of their own and it is the same for children. That is why it is essential for their development and self esteem that they are treated as individuals and are also called by their given name not a nickname.

Ways of increasing income

- Sell something, anything that is no longer used, on Ebay.

- Take in a boarder, there is a rent-a-room scheme where you are allowed a certain amount of tax-free income before you need to declare it for tax so this is potentially lucrative. However, if you are a single female, insist on references. We do know of one woman who let a room to a lodger, only to be raped and held prisoner so either insist on another female only (but don't say so out loud) or make sure you have at least three references, including one official one, for the prospective lodger. You must make sure these are references and not testimonials. A reference is a letter that the applicant does not see. A testimonial is something she or he may bring with them. If they are cagey about supplying referees' names and addresses, don't have them in your home.

- Do some overtime at work.

- Take a second part-time job.

- Do some private tutoring. Even if you are not a qualified teacher you could still do something but remember you may need to register with the authorities if you have access to children. If you are doing private tutoring in someone else's home make sure that an adult is always near by, that way both you and the child is protected.

- If you are in work, look for better paid work or ask for a raise

- Become a consultant to sell any expertise that you have.

Don't just rely on my list, it is important that you write up your own. As a writer I have a certain level of experience to draw on which maybe totally different to yours so scour your past for opportunities to utilise the skills and experience you have. Remember, these are early and probably temporary measures, they are not forever. However, there are cases of people who have started part-time work to raise money and found it far more lucrative that the day job. They have given up the day job to work full time on what was a part-time job. I know of a writer who was a Deputy Head but gave it up to be a full-time writer on the TV soap *Emmerdale*. He has also written many episodes of the *Archers* for Radio 4. Your life's journey could also change in this way.

Rule one: Do not give up the day job: despite what I have said above about the writer who is an ex-deputy head, *do not give up the day job*. This is your bread and butter. I stress this because some financial gurus will exhort you to work for yourself at any cost. This is easy to say but has potentially unacceptable consequences. A number of Australians were encouraged by people to give up their day jobs and start their own businesses. The following year there was a slew of bankruptcies across the same area of Australia that correlated extremely well with the tour route this financial guru had taken. Now this may be chance but we are not convinced. Self-employment is not for everyone, so Rule Number 1, do not give up the day job.

Rule two: Desk research. Cost out everything first before you spend a single penny. Do not spend one penny on books or biz ops or anything else in order to raise money. This programme is about getting you out of debt. That may sound a little hypocritical since you have bought this book, but you will see dozens of 'get rich quick schemes', trust me they do not work. Google is a great search engine to find information, you really do not need to spend hundreds of pounds and they often do cost hundreds of pounds on a biz op. One of the worst cases I have ever heard of was a husband and wife team who opened a restaurant. They spent around £250,000 on starting the business and only when they had done so did they 'discover' that if they had every table in the restaurant full three times per night, seven nights per week, they would only just break even. In other words they could never make a profit. This was foolhardy and could have been avoided by a piece of desk research. All that was needed was to make a simple calculation: what is the break-even point? You are in the position where you need to increase income, so as we have already said do not give up the day job. However, if you intend to start some sort of part-time business to increase money then you need to ask yourself the following questions.

1	What community/audience can I get to and what are their needs?
2	What product or service can I develop for this community/audience?
3	Who from this community will buy my service/product? (If you say 'everyone' you need a reality check.)

There is *no* product or service that is bought by everyone. Even holy books like the Bible or the Koran have a limited sale. There is similarly no population or audience rather than at a niche level that will buy every product or service from a source, so you do need to know how many products or service sessions you need to deliver to break even.

Rule three: Look for free resources, such as Google free business cards and use them. There are plenty of other free resources, if you are starting a part-time enterprise then try Googling for a business plan for that business. Do make the effort to talk to people in that business before you spend one penny.

Rule four: Getting out in your spare time to find extra income. You have to make the effort. It is all to easy to claim being tired but the effort now will be worth it.

Rule five: Quality – be the best and take this quality into the day job. What we are talking about here is an expansion of your consciousness. Think what it means to be the best. It is to be respected and admired. Why should it not happen to you? Taking this into the day job can only increase your standing and can lead to an increase in your income, when management becomes aware of what you have done to add value to your organisation.

Expanding your consciousness

My grandmother was intrigued when she heard I was going to college. In North Wales, grandmother is Nain (pronounced Nine) and grandfather is Taid (pronounced Tide).

She said 'Graham, I know you are going to college and I know you will spend three years there but what will you be when you come out?'

I said, 'I'll be a teacher Nain.'

She said, 'Don't be silly, people like us don't do jobs like that'.

For Nain this was against everything she understood, she had been smart enough to achieve a pass to go to the grammar school but it was during the First World War and she was not allowed to go and anyway at the time it was thought to be a waste to educate girls. (It is not, women form the hub of a family and can have a wonderful positive influence on all members of a family, not just children. This is a great way to develop the people in a family, educate the mother and she will educate the rest of the family.) Nain wasn't able to expand her consciousness enough to accept that this was now a reality; it was just too far at that time.

You have to expand your consciousness, why shouldn't you be wealthy? You have as much right as, say, David Beckham. Maybe you will not do it playing soccer but there are other ways forward. So make sure you are not limiting your thinking by avoiding expanding your consciousness.

If, like me, your heritage is from the working class then you will encounter prejudice. I worked in an office in Somerset as I said earlier and one man came to visit. When he heard

I had a Masters degree, he said: 'Yes, but it's not an Oxbridge degree is it?' I said 'No, it is an Open University Masters Degree'. 'Exactly', he sniffed, 'not an Oxbridge degree'. When I told him I had to pass exams and write a thesis for my Masters degree he was astonished. You may not be aware that for many if not all Oxbridge masters degrees, all he had had to do was send off a cheque for a certain amount and his MA was a formality. The argument is that Oxbridge degrees are far harder than undergraduate degrees from elsewhere. I cannot comment on that but I have great pride in my Open University degree and in the Open University itself. (If you are thinking about doing an OU course, *do it*, it changed my life and it can change yours, it really can.) My point is that you have to expect ignorant people like this and not to be put off balance, it is very easy to lose confidence in yourself and your abilities, don't. This man had studied at Oxford and then spent his working life in Oxford, I certainly was not going to let him get under my skin and you should not let any other people like this get under your skin.

You need to understand that *you* are responsible for improving your own life. Yes, you can audition for TV shows like the X Factor or try winning the lottery but what is this about? I suggest that what people want is to change their lives for the better without the personal effort required. Real change comes from within, real security comes from within not externally. In fact, look at the people who have won the talent shows that have been on UK TV in recent years, they by and large have been in the trade anyway. Connie Fisher, Lee Meads and Jodie Prenger were all experienced performers before they won the competitions in which they took part. They had all completed a long hard apprenticeship, they had, as the phrase goes 'studied hard and paid their dues'. The change in their lives had come from within not externally. Change that is going to improve the self comes from within.

I wanted a better life so I joined the Open University and slogged with them for six years before joining Cardiff University and slogging with them for ten years, change has to come from within. The self is who you perceive yourself to be, it is a composition of your thoughts and beliefs based on your experiences in life and how you have reacted to them. It is essential for your notion of self to change if you are going to develop. If this notion of self does not change then the reality will be that you will continue to behave as you did previously and eventually you will continue to behave in the same way and this will lead you back to incurring debt. If you are reading this and saying 'Graham, I can't change my consciousness', then I guarantee you will not do so. It is only when you see the new you that you will move towards that person.

Look at where you physically are now and see a series of silhouettes in front of you. The silhouette is the person you are going to become, but you have to walk up to that silhouette and inhabit it, you have to move forward and you have to make the effort to move forward. Try it now, think about the person ahead of you, that is who you are going to become. What does she or he see at this moment, how good do they look? I bet they are more confident than you are right now, this is the person you are going to become. So the way to move forward is to take action. You need to develop an action plan that reflects your future including your financial future.

The Repayment Plan

9

The rapid repayment plan (RRP)

Now we are at a major stage in the programme the Back to the black rapid repayment plan. The beauty of this plan is that it gives you a second chance, you are given a second chance to get back into the driving seat and take control of your life. Instead of the marketeers and businesses in the high street controlling who you are and what you buy, by going through this programme you really are designing your life again and taking control.

Remember the culture of the marketeers is designed to take money out of your pocket or purse and put it into their accounts. This programme gives you the chance to ignore their approach to living, what social scientists call 'enculturation' and create your own approach. This will take some effort and probably some time but it is essential for your future well-being. You have to put the effort into avoid increasing your debt, avoiding impulse buying and not being seduced by mail shots. That way you are creating your own culture, your own approach to how cash should be managed and how it does and does not come into your home.

The marketeers want you to be in debt, they want you to have the latest must-haves, even if you can't afford them, because that way they get you into debt and then they make money in two ways. Firstly on the sale of the product they have persuaded you to buy and secondly on the interest on the payments. Let me ask you this Would you pay £32.50 for a £25 jumper from a well-known high street store? This is a serious question, would you really pay £7.50 more for the same product? That is exactly what you do when you use credit. What about a car, would you pay

£6,500 for a used car worth £5,000? You do when you use credit, can you see why I have kept on about this, because when you use credit they love it. They are getting far more from you than the initial sale. **Remember: they agree to lend you money and you agree to make them wealthy**.

What if there was another way, a way of paying off debt and in the long term ensuring that there is money to buy things and that you never need to be in debt? There is another approach, it is the Back to the black rapid repayment plan.

This is a fundamental plank in the Back to the black programme and without it you are sunk but remember it is a plan. This plan will help you create the future of prosperity and abundance you desire, it will help you plan to get to where you want to be. However, you must ensure that the repayment is *not* at the expense of the quality of your life. This will kill the central point of this programme and probably lead you further into debt. Why do I say that? Quite simply because that is what I did. I can remember walking into Smiths in Loughborough and buying a book. I had hundreds of books at home and did I really need another, no I did not *but* it made me feel better. I was alone and miserable and wanted some cheer and so I fell into old habits and if there is no joy in your life you will do the same and relapse into spending too much. You may be thinking 'Graham, you really have lost it now,' actually I have not. The purpose of this programme is to improve *your* life not that of your creditors. They do *not* own you, they own the debt and you are *not* your debt. You are living for you *not* for your creditors, you need to understand something very important:

You come first, your creditors come second.

It does not matter who they are, they are *not* as important as you and you must never lose sight of that fact. Type out

the sentence YOU COME FIRST, YOUR CREDITORS
COME SECOND on a word processor and place it
somewhere in your home, where you will regularly see it.
When I had to do things like this I usually wrote them in
Welsh when I was living in England so that if anyone else
saw it, it stayed personal to me. So if you have a second
language don't be afraid to use it for personal matters.
When I worked in the Somerset office, one woman asked
why I always wrote in my notebook in Welsh. (I am a
Welsh learner.) I answered that you either 'Use a language
or lose a language'. She replied, 'But we don't know what
you are saying'. This was, in my view, the height of ill
manners, why does she need to read my private notebook?
So if you have a second language then use it and be proud
that you have a second language, it is a fundamental part of
who you are as a human being.

Now it is time to create the Back to the black rapid
repayment plan. As you will remember, we have already
designed a spending plan that links with your spending
record. If you need to, read back over this in the previous
chapter and make sure it is clear. Remember we had the
80:19:1 rule, we have use the 80 and the 1, 10% of the 19 is
also used up (remember we are using this to create your
contingency fund) so we have 9% of your total take-home
income to play with. In the example we used in earlier
chapters this is £108. The way to work this out is easy, 9%
is 0.09 (notice the 9 is in the second column on the right
after the decimal point, if it were in the first column that
would be 90%).

So then we worked out $0.09 \times £1,200$ and got £108. This is
allocated to debt repayment and will be spent but when at
some point in the future the debts are all paid off, this
money is *not* for spending and must not be allocated to the
spending record. When the debts are paid off this money
will create a new pot of loot for *investments*. But more of
that later.

You need to multiply your take-home pay by 0.09 and that will give you an accurate picture of exactly how much you have for debt repayment. Right now, from our example, we have £108 to spend paying off debt. Go to your debt drawer and bring out your list of creditors and your envelopes. If you have not done it already then do it now. You need a list of *all* of your debts and who they are owed to and it must be accurate. When you have finished writing the list add up the total debt. You now need to work out the creditor percentage, this is the percentage each creditor is due from the 9%. It is an easy calculation, take the creditor amount and divide it by the total debt and then multiply by 100, this will tell you the total debt.

Say I owe Dad £1,000 out of a total of debt of £8,800, then dad's percentage is:

$$(1000/8800) \times 100 = 11.36\%$$

This answer is the proportion of the debt repayment that dad gets each month. You need to do this calculation for every debtor and make a list. Our list looks like this:

Person/organisation	Total debt	Share
Dad	£1,000	11.36%
MasterCard	£3,000	34.1%
Home entertainment centre	£4,800	54.55%

For the purposes of this example we have kept the number of creditors small but realistic. The largest debt is the home entertainment centre and therefore this gets the largest part of the RRP.

In our example we have £108 to pay all this off. You might be shouting at the book now saying, 'Graham, get real, this will never work. I have £50,000 worth of debts, not a measly eight grand or so.' But it will work, stay with me and you will see what I mean. It really does not matter what the size of the debt is, this will work.

Now you need to make another list for the RRP.

Person/organisation	Total debt	Share	Payment
Dad	£1,000	11.36%	
MasterCard	£3,000	34.1%	
Home entertainment centre	£4,800	54.55%	

Now calculate the share percentage of the available amount, namely your 9%, which in our example is £108, so for this payment Dad gets 11.36%. So that is 11.36/100 × 108 which comes to £12.27 per month. This is the amount we are going to pay Dad. Now take Dad's total debt of £1,000 and divide it by £12.27 and this will tell you how many months you need to pay until the debt is clear (this is 81.49 months). This six years and just over nine months. Do the same for the rest of your debtors. Now don't worry at this stage if this seems a long time, I have another trick up my sleeve and anyway six years nine months is a lot less than a lifetime in debt.

For MasterCard the percentage is 34.1% so work out 34.1% of £108 and this is the amount to pay back to MasterCard, so 34.1/100 × 108 = £36.83(this is 81.45 months to pay, in fact slightly less than the time taken to pay Dad).

For the home entertainment centre the debt is £3,000 and the proportion of the available cash in the rapid repayment plan is 54.55% so work out 54.55/100 × 108 = £58.91, (this is 81.4 months). Look at the power of this technique. It means that in less than seven years you will have paid back *all* of your debts in this scenario. It may take you longer or it may take you less.

Here is an alternative strategy, I am one of the fortunates who have a great family and if I owed my Dad, I know what he would say, 'Pay off the others first son'. So what would that do? It adds another 5.68% to each of the other bills. So MasterCard now becomes 39.78%. Therefore 39.78/100 × 108 = £42.96, the time period to pay is 69 months.

The home entertainment payment becomes £65.05 per
month. The time period is 73 months, so in around six
years both of these are paid and then Dad can be paid *but*
he would be paid at £108 per month which will
undoubtedly have gone up in the meantime as your pay
increased over time. So there is a choice for you to make.
The principle is the same, you are allocating funds for a
specific purpose and ensuring that you get that payment
made to them. This is the amount we pay back to the
people from whom we bought the home entertainment
centre and commit to paying every month.

You need to go through the same process for all of your
debts, work out the proportion of debt to the available debt
repayment and commit to paying it every month.

OK, you may say that this is just pence and that you have
huge bills, but it does not matter. It will not take forever, **as
long as you incur no new debt**. It is only by not using
credit that you can ever hope to get a grip on your
spending and if you do use a credit card then you *must* pay
it off in full before the end of the month. One good way of
doing this is every time you use the credit card, when you
get home write a cheque immediately for that amount and
add it to your daily spending record. That way it is
accounted for and will not bite you on the proverbial at the
end of the month.

Think about the process, you have changed your life. I
started this book by saying I wanted to change your life.
Actually that was not quite true, I wanted to give you the
tools to change your life and this is one of those major tools
that is life changing. Look at what has happened (assuming
you have worked along with me then you have changed
your life), you are now getting *out* of debt not getting *into*
debt. This is a huge achievement and one of which you can
be justifiably proud.

A pound a month

I once did some work for a magazine in Leicester didn't get paid. Anyway to cut a long story short I took him to court for payment. He had published the work I had written and as a writer this is a major plank of how I earn a living. The judgement went my way and he was ordered to pay but – and this is the point of the story – at £1 a month. I had no choice I had to accept it and so will your creditors. If that is all you can afford then that is all you can afford and you have no need to feel embarrassed about it. Clearly it will take time to repay all off the money you owe but as someone once said every journey begins with a single step. The creditors may and probably will try to bully you whatever your level of payments. but you need to hold the line. We did hear of a company who were very slow at paying and when someone rang up demanding immediate payment, a very 'theatrical' male said, 'You don't seem to understand how we work here, at the end of the month we put all of the bills into a hat and then pick out a few that we can pay, and if you are not nicer to me you won't even get into the hat' and then he slammed down the phone. Look at who holds the power here, it is *not* them it is you. You have their money in the form of credit and you are agreeing to pay it back but at a pace that suits *you* not them, I have said this before *you* come first, then your creditors.

Some repayment plans are not perfect and in the same way that I suggest that if your Dad is like mine you can put him last on the repayment scheme *but* you must pay Dad as well as everyone else. The other thing to consider is that if you have a number of credit card bills and you have some with horrendously high interest rates, then you may consider paying these off first. In this case then your RRP needs to pay the minimum required per month (if that is possible, see the next chapter for help if you cannot meet the minimum), for the other cards and pay this one off as quickly as possible. This is a judgement you need to make

but stand your ground and do not be bowed by companies
threatening litigation or solicitors (we will discuss
correspondence in the next chapter).

An interest(ing) question

What about interest payments? In the ideal RRP you would
be paying back principle (the original amount borrowed)
and interest. If this is impossible, then go through your
spending plan and see where you can shave off more money
to go to debt repayment *but* do not shave off the categories
that lead to you enjoying life. Assuming these are reasonable
and not disproportionate to your income, then these are
what makes us human, these are the areas of life that means
we can have some fun. Remember what Noel Edmonds said
in his book, 'We are here for a good time not a long time'.

It may be that you think your situation is irretrievable, but
you are wrong, it is not. However, I am convinced of one
thing, you will not get rid of these debts by incurring more
debt. *Do not touch loan sharks*; they will have the clothes off
your back. I have heard of loan sharks who really do send
the heavies around and they are *not* nice people. If you are
a victim of a loan shark then go to Citizens Advice Bureau
and get help. This will not cost you anything and they can
guide you. If all else fails get this debt paid off urgently. The
problem with loan sharks is they are always circling. We
heard of one couple in Glasgow who borrowed £60 to get
married during the 1980s and have been paying over £30
per month ever since. The interest rate was well over
10,000%. Think about it, for every pound they borrowed
they are paying back £10,000, so their wedding will
eventually cost them over £60 000. The last we heard was
that Scottish legal officers were examining the contract and
referring it to law, because it was deemed an illegal contract
and they were waiting for a legal judgement. We wish the
couple well, they deserve it. You do not want to be in a
similar position.

Moving debt

Shifting the debt from one place is another way to relieve the pressure of high interest rates. Notice in this case you do not reduce the debt principle but you do reduce the interest rate that you are paying, so the overall repayment of principle and interest will be less. You are not getting new debt, you are simply changing creditors.

So be strong because you are strong, you are no longer getting deeper in debt, every day means you are getting closer towards a debt free life, towards total freedom.

10 The Future You

Talking to creditors

So how do you feel? Welcome to the new you. You have started to create a new life for yourself and now is the time to enjoy that feeling. If you have worked through the programme you should feel strong and your self-esteem should be high. Now is the time to start spreading the news and talking to your creditors. Don't panic, you can do this, it is straightforward. Look at how far you have come already in the Back to the black programme, look at how much you have changed.

You are now in control, you have come through an experience where you have been encouraged to reflect on past actions and assimilate new actions into your behaviour. You have been given new tools and shown how to use them and by now you should be feeling great, so there is nothing to worry about.

One word of warning. Regardless of what you have been like in the past from now on you must be scrupulously honest with your creditors. Remember at the same time as working your rapid repayment plan you are also building your contingency fund and your POM fund. This means you have protection for when disaster strikes and you have the POM fund to pay for the irregular debt. The back to the black programme is therefore a three-pronged attack that traps debt and destroys it by removing it from your life. With all of these tools and this new-found power you have no need to lie. By being honest you will benefit and so will your creditors.

Get in touch

It is important that you take the initiative, and get in touch with your creditors. By doing this you are setting up a record, you are taking control by taking action. Be explicit about your situation with them *but* do not put yourself down. Don't say, 'Well, I have been very silly…'. All this will do is diminish you in front of them. It is far better to use phrases like 'Due to my circumstances…', especially if you left college or university with debt, as many young people are forced to do. Do tell the creditor that you regret the situation, but that you are committed to paying them in full and make sure you tell them that you have a spending plan, and are spending accordingly. Don't mention the POM or contingency fund as they may insist you raid that to pay that money to them. Remember what we said *you* come first, so keep that quiet. Regardless of how they act, keep calm, and don't be threatened.

I once owed the electricity board money because they had not been to read the meter. I offered to read the meter for them but they declined, because I had read it the last three times and they needed their own staff to check it. So they said I had to allow them entry, I said fine, make an appointment after 4 pm when I would be back from school, but this was the sticking point. On the phone I was told that 'We don't work after 4 o'clock, you will leave a key at the office and we will let ourselves in.

The woman on the phone really lost it when I declined. Now call me old fashioned if you like, but if someone is in my house I want to know what is going on and that means being there. She yelled at me down the phone and threatened to cut me off. I replied that if I was cut off I would make sure all the local media were aware of what they had done. The local media would relish a story of the little guy being bullied by the corporation. The result? About a week later there was a knock on the door and the area manager came to read the meter. It would have been to capitulate but I stood my ground and in this case, they still chose to bully me even though I was *not* in arrears. So stay calm and steady regardless of what the other person does or says.

Dealing with organisations

One tip when dealing with organisations, is to make sure you get your contact's name at the start of the conversation and write it down (we'll talk more about this later). But it is important that you log all names, dates and times of conversations. The first person you talk to is probably a low-level employee and has probably limited authority. Now think of what you are doing here. You are telling them that you will be paying x amount, according to your RRP. They will probably respond 'That is not enough'. You say, 'that is all I have'. They start getting shirty with you.

A better approach is to tell the low-level employee, this is what I want you to tell your manager and then explain how much you are going to pay and how long you estimate it will be before the total is paid. Now is the time to stick your neck out by at least three metres and ask for a reduction in interest. If you are paying a rate over 5% ask for at least a 2% reduction. They can only say no and you will be no worse off but if they say yes, you save 2% on the deal. Think about it, it is *not* their money they are collecting, by this I mean it is not their personal money so they can pass the request on.

When you have made the request, ask the employee to ask his or her manager to write back with their answer to the request. It is vital that you get this answer on paper and keep it in a log. One of my colleagues once told me how his bank wrote to him and asked him to explain why he and his wife were *not* paying a fee on their account and by the bank's reckoning they (the bank) were owed two years' bank charges. Veronica went straight to her file and pulled out a letter from the bank copied it and sent it to the bank. The letter said they would never be charged, and they were not, at least for the two years. The bank did start charging from then on, so sensibly they moved banks.

If you get an unhelpful letter back then get back on the phone and ask to talk to the person who sent it. Remember to keep calm and insist that you are responding to their letter. Stick to your guns. Do not capitulate, tell them what you can afford and point out that they are getting their money back. If they take a hard stance you will not be able to pay anything. The worst-case scenario is that you end up in court. They will be on sticky ground when you explain to the court that you intended to pay them and that they were awkward about it, so don't worry about that one. The chances of their taking action against you are slim and they would be regarded as foolish by many courts to take this action. Remember you are in charge not them, you are not the inferior here, you are taking control of a situation and communicating it with them. This is a business deal where you both want the same thing, you want to pay the money back and they want their money back so in that sense it is a win-win. You know what you can and can't pay. Your job is to tell them that and by all means quote this book. Do tell them 'I have based this on a strategy developed from a number of American schemes by Dr Graham Lawler in his book *Back to the black*'. Again this is a win win for you and me, by quoting an academic you gain credibility and I get a plug for this book (well it is my bread and butter!)

Most creditors are willing to engage in this sort of agreement for one simple reason. If you default on the loan and they get nothing, they do not achieve the objective of getting their money back.

The contact log

It is essential that you keep a log of all contacts you make with a creditor. It is vital that you know precisely what was discussed. This log can also be a powerful defence against a possible legal action by a creditor. The log should be in two parts. In the first part you need to note all personal meetings and telephone conversations. During the meeting or phone conversation you should make notes and you should always end the meeting with a summary of what was agreed and ensure the other person agrees with you that this is a fair summary of what was said. Then make a note after the meeting or telephone conversation of what was agreed under the heading of 'memorandum of understanding'. This should then be filed in the second half of your log and references to the call or meeting in the first half. A copy should be sent to the person with whom you have had the meeting. Remember it is essential to summarise the main points of agreement at the end of the meeting and then to immediately write up the memorandum of understanding. Sign and date the copy you send to the other person and include a second copy for him/her to sign and return to you. Your covering letter must say that this is what you want. Ensure you keep a copy of the covering letter in your file. Keep a record of all correspondence from them to you and date it as it comes in. If you do ask for and get a reduced interest rate on your debt, ensure that you keep this on record as you may need it for proof at a later date.

Do not sign any forms and return them unless you are absolutely sure what it is you are signing and make sure you keep copies of them. If you are unsure of the forms they are asking you to sign, send them back *unsigned* with a query letter asking for clarification. You cannot be criticised for asking for information. One lady we know was asked if she would be guarantor for her son and his girlfriend and baby's rent, she agreed. When she was presented with the forms she was about to sign when she was gently asked did she understand what it meant. She said not really. When it was explained that if the son did not pay his rent, she would be obligated to pay it, she flew into a fit, no one had explained it in terms that she understood. Make sure you understand and don't sign if you do not understand.

You should also be aware that very often one side of a company or organisation does not know what another side is doing.

Your creditor list

In the last chapter we discussed how to calculate your rapid repayment plan. Now is the time to communicate that repayment plan to your creditor and record it as we have just discussed. Do not be surprised if they write back and immediately reject the plan. *Do not* be disturbed by this, send the amount you said you would send and ensure every month that you send the same amount. It is essential that you are not cowed by some large institution. Remember *you* are in control here. **Warning**: if you miss one payment it will be recorded that you are unreliable.

Your pay-off record (POR)

You need an A4 folder with A4 paper. Put each creditor's name at the top of a separate page. Then on the page write down each payment as you make it, even if it is only £1. Then subtract the payment from the balance and write the new balance on the page. This is an important tool in your armoury of debt repayment; it has a specific function to support you in your journey. This is your source of energy. When you are feeling low use this as a battery of energy that tells you how well you are doing. It is vital in your move towards a new life. It is the key to liquidating your debts.

Your liquidation record

Your rapid repayment plan is not set in stone. As you earn more you may add more to the sums you are repaying and therefore shorten the repayment term. When the day comes when you are sending the final payment to a creditor (and it will come), you can then celebrate. You do this by recording it in your liquidation record. This is a list of all debts that are paid off and the final date on which they are paid. When you are sending the final payment make sure you include a letter that states 'This is the final payment for the debt of [*state value*] owed by [*your name*]. I declare this debt is now paid in full and therefore no further payments will be forthcoming from me', and then sign and date the letter. Congratulations, you have signed off your first debt. Doesn't that feel good?

When the final debt is paid you can regard yourself as a major success *but* you must not absorb the money in the repaid repayment plan into daily spending. At this happy stage it is time to introduce you to a choice.

The first choice is to pay off all remaining secured debt, like the mortgage. The second choice is to say 'I will live with having secured debt like the mortgage and I will use this money to invest', in other words to do as we said earlier in the book, to buy assets, not liabilities. You have to decide what you are most comfortable with. When I was younger it was to have more investments but following the mess the banks have made and how they led us into the post-2007 world, now I want to clear the mortgage. (Why is it that we have bailed out these banks and yet some of these guys are still in position? Shouldn't some of them be serving time at Her Majesty's pleasure? Surely this was criminality in action? But I digress.)

If you have paid off all of the debt then well done but keep saving the money from the RRP and put it into a pot of loot. If you have a mortgage, use it to pay off the mortgage at a far faster rate than you were previously doing. If you are renting, then I suggest you consider saving a deposit for a mortgage. 'Ah, Graham, you say, 'but house prices fell after the 2007 banking scandal didn't they?' Yes they did and this means it is probably one of the best times to buy a house since previously they were overvalued. In reality the days of 100% mortgages and easy credit have gone, we are in a far stricter financial regime now. In January 2009 I visited the Canary Islands and I noticed how quiet all the shops were. Demand for goods is at an all time low across the whole of Europe and the Canaries and from press reports across the USA too, so it means that this is a buyers' market. Now the shoe is on the other foot: you are not a creditor any more, you have money to spend and people who need to shift their homes are often in quite needy stakes, they are called distressed buyers. So this is a possibility for you *but* you need to have a good deposit at least 10%, so you do have some savings to build up yet.

Rainy days and Mondays

If you are old enough to remember the 1970s you will remember the Carpenters and the late Karen Carpenter's rendition of a song which had a line 'rainy days and Mondays always get me down'. (If you don't know this song, try You Tube, she is probably on there singing it.) Saving for a rainy day can also get you down. My good friend Deborah Harty (see www.deborahharty.co.uk) says she often gets clients in her practice who are moaning that they are broke and cannot afford things but have thousands of pounds saved. When Deborah gently points out that they in fact do have money they often reply 'But that is for a rainy day'. This rainy day has become a fictional catastrophe some time in the future that you are waiting to happen and it can become a self fulfilling prophecy. Because you are waiting for it to happen, it somehow magically happens. But wait, we have already covered this one, it is your contingency fund which we discussed earlier. If there is an emergency you have at least three months' pay in the kitty to tide you over, so why are you saving for the rainy day? This develops what is called poverty mentality, we start to live poor because we think we are poor. In fact we are far better off in many ways more than most people in the world. Britain may have lousy weather at times but the rest of the experience of living in Britain is pretty good in my view so rejoice and celebrate the fact that the God you may or may not believe in has led you to live in one of the best (if not the best) countries in the world.

So where are you now?

As we come to the end of our journey together I wa
first of all say well done. If you are at this point in t
and have worked through all of the structures and us
of the tools I have explained then you really have cha
your life. You are no longer a debtor, you are now a s   ...

So now is the time to get a little dreamy, as long as there is
a certain realism in your dreams. Get yourself a cup of
coffee and a pad of paper and then start to dream...what
would your ideal life be like? Go on, dare to dream. Where
would you live? What sort of house would it be? What sort
of job would you do? Would it be the same job as you do
now? What kind of car would you drive?

In my case I was very fortunate to have a supportive
partner, in my wife Judith. When we went to through this
stage she said, 'In your ideal life would you still be a
teacher?' Without hesitating I said 'No, I want to write,' and
that is what I now do. OK it may not be your cup of tea
but for me, I am living my dream. I love getting up in the
morning and going down to my study. I am a publisher and
writer, in that I publish other people's books and I write
and publish my own books. I have been described as leisure
phobic because I don't play golf, I rarely go to the pub, why
should I? I am having a blast every day. In my study first
thing in the morning I have the Radio 4 *Today* programme
and then from 9 o'clock (I always start early, bit of a lark
rather than a nightingale) the man with the dulcet tones on
Classic FM takes me through the morning. Occasionally I
go out to colleges and universities to meet colleagues and I
go to Frankfurt and London to the book shows. I have the
joy of living in a beautiful part of the country, and if you
have never been to North Wales then do come you will be
warmly welcomed. You will hear people speaking Welsh but
don't be fretful about that, it is their language (Judith is
English and doesn't speak a word of Welsh and she has
been warmly welcomed by the local community) and I

highly recommend the hotels in Abergele, Llanfair TH, Colwyn Bay and Llandudno and equally there are wonderful bed and breakfast accommodation places to stay, google North Wales tourism for more details. Look it up on a map and come on over.

OK I am not wealthy and I did take a huge hit in salary when I finished teaching altogether, but I am two stone lighter and frankly far happier. As a teacher I had got to head of department level and then I had a senior position in a college and then finished teaching at a university (which was fun) but for me I had got up the ladder only to find it was against the wrong wall and a career change did change my life for the better. So my days are a blast, the work I do is challenging and fun and I love it. This is what I want for you. In my case I took a lot of courses with the Open University and developed myself and you can do the same. I have to say that every course I took helped me grow in confidence and I hope this book has done the same for you.

The point is that within reason you can have everything you want. I say within reason for a good point, I recently watched my team (there is only one Manchester United) on TV and was imagining being out there scoring. Now this is nonsense because I am a middle-aged man pushing 50 and frankly far too old. I am not suggesting that you should aim to emulate my life but I am saying that I am living my dream and you could and should live your own dream. I once taught a boy called Kevin, he looked at me in disgust and said 'You're not a man unless you work with a shovel'. Kevin will be in his forties now, I hope he is happy with his shovel but I can guarantee one thing, working with a shovel will not make him wealthy, it is only by using the notions I have explained in this book that you will clear your debts and make money.

The ideal spending plan

So with this in mind, now is the time to dare to dream.

The best place to start is with your ideal spending plan.
This is not the spending plan you followed or are still
following to get out of debt. This is your spending plan for
your ideal life. What would it be? The only way to create
your ideal life is to imagine it and then work towards
achieving it. You really can do it. By following the Back to
the black programme you have or still are paying off debt.
The dare to dream part is you way to create the next stage
in your life. So in your ideal life write the following
categories.

- Career.
- Money.
- Personal possessions.
- Personal development/education.
- Relationships.
- Play activities.
- Recreation.

Use these categories as headings and then under each
heading write down a scenario that would be your ideal. Let
go of your inhibitions, don't be limited like Kevin and his
shovel, let your wishes go wild *but* do it in the present
tense. The only way to make your life better is to imagine
it, to envisage it, we become what we think about. If you
are constantly thinking about poverty you will become poor,
if you think about both the good things you have in your
life now and the good things you could have, you will open
yourself up to having them. Look at what you have written,
here is a possible example:

> *I earn £75,000 per year and have been out of debt for five
> years. I have a wonderful relationship with . . . and I make
> it a point of being positive in my relationship with him/
> her. Every day I make a point of finding something positive*

to say to him/her. By being supportive like this I see him/ her developing their own sense of self-esteem and we go forward together as a couple. I have an investment portfolio of £250,000 which pays me dividends per year. I work a four' day week through choice and I both value my work and the people I work with. I holiday in the Caribbean in the winter and in Europe in the summer. At the weekends I play golf and work with . . . in the garden.

Life is to be enjoyed not endured.
Dr Graham Lawler
(aka the radio broadcaster Mr Educator)

By creating your image of your own personal dream, by having a clear picture of where you want to live and the lifestyle you want, you will be guided towards making decisions that takes you closer towards it, you are moving towards it. Take the time and make the effort to redraft your ideal life, your subconscious will begin to relax and open up to possibilities. Make it fun because it is fun, it is not work. The point of doing this is to reveal to yourself the kind of life you really would like to have and to break the chains of the old thinking that binds you to the past. In my case I kept teaching part-time for a number of years because I was afraid that I couldn't make it just by writing, I even used to dream about having one foot in one boat and the second foot in another boat and then one night in the recurring dream I stepped fully into the second boat. In the morning when I told Judith she said quite eloquently, 'OK now you are ready to move forward to the next stage of your life' (she is a wise woman).

Remember you are not committed to this vision in total. If you review it every two weeks you will find that you have changed and that you no longer wish to have that. Don't think that just because you wrote it down it is essential that you have to do it. It is not, you are not dealing with something set in stone, it is your future and you have to create it.

So there we are, at the end of our journey together you should now have paid off or be in the process of paying off debts. You have the tools to create the sort of life you want and by the time you read this I should have launched the Back to the black website. We are going to develop more products to help you with money management including an audio version of this book. The audio version will have more material in it so it will not simply be a duplicate of what you already have. So, via the website (www.aber-publishing.co.uk) do let me know how you are getting on, it would be great to have case studies for future versions of this book or simply to put on the website. Don't worry, we will keep your name and personal details private.

The 2007 credit crunch changed the financial world and we have to become savvy and protect ourselves, that way we can enjoy the better things of life, have great relationships with loved ones, family and friends and sleep well and that is what we all deserve.

All the best

Graham

Glossary

Assets. Think of these as investments, they bring money to you because they usually (but not always) increase in value. So gold is an investment, it usually goes up in value over time. A car is **not** an asset because it does **down** in value.

Annual fee. A fee paid by you to the manager of your investment or life insurance/pension policy. This fee is payable very year.

APR (annual percentage rate). The rate to use when comparing different products. Lenders must tell you what the APR rate is before you take credit.

Bad debt. A debt that is cancelled or written off because the creditor is not able to pay or the cost of getting the money is more than the money itself.

Bank charges. These are charges the bank may be applying to you to handle your account.

Bankruptcy. This is where a person cannot pay their debts, and is served with a bankruptcy order by a court. The petition to the court can be filed either by the person concerned or by his/her creditors. The Official Receiver then makes an inquiry into the debtor's affairs.

Contingency fund. This is catastrophe money – a fund of money you have saved so that in the event of a major problem, such as losing a job, you have something to fall back on until you get back on your feet. You must keep this account liquid (see below).

Creditors. These are the people and/or organisations you whom you owe money.

Credit card. A card that allows you to purchase goods and services and then pay for them within a fixed period without having to pay interest.

Current account. The account you draw money from (also known as a cheque account).

Debt. Money owed by an individual or company to another individual or company.

Debit card. This type of card works in the same way as a credit card, but money is taken from your account immediately.

Debt consolidation. All debts are amalgamated into one bigger debt and it is paid off over a longer period of time. This usually means that the monthly outgoings are lower but the length of time is longer, so you will probably pay back more. You need to do some calculations to check this.

Estate. This is the total of everything that you own minus everything you owe. If you are making a will, make sure you have some idea of the value of your estate now and what it might be in the future. It is worth considering getting independent advice on tax planning if you have a larger than average estate.

Flexible loan. An account where you can draw money when you need it, to an agreed limit. (Now you are using the Back to the Black plan, you do not need this type of account.)

Interest. A fee added to the amount borrowed for the privilege of borrowing someone else's money.

Liabilities. These are possessions that go down in value, they take money away from you. A car is a liability since it reduces in value and costs money to run and maintain.

Liquid funds. Easily accessible funds when you need money fast. They are not tied up in some way and you can retrieve your money quickly.

POM (Peace of Mind account). The account you pay money into every month so that when you receive a utility bill (electricity/gas/water rates, etc), you use this account to pay the bill(s).

Rapid repayment plan (RRP). A plan to pay off your debts and make a fresh debt-free start.

Index